FLORIDA AT WAR
FORTS AND BATTLES

DONALD D. SPENCER

Schiffer Publishing Ltd
4880 Lower Valley Road Atglen, Pennsylvania 19310

Other Schiffer Books By The Author:

Cape Canaveral,
978-0-7643-3616-4, $29.99

A History of the Alligator: Florida's Favorite Reptile,
978-0-7643-3083-4, $24.99

Other Schiffer Books on Related Subjects:

Chesapeake Bay in the Civil War,
978-0-7643-3592-1, $29.99

Civil War Re-enactment,
0-8874-0949-0, $19.95

DEDICATION

To my grandsons,
Todd and Keith Merritt

Photo Credits: Donald Spencer's postcard and photograph collection form the base for this book, augmented by photographs from the Florida State Photographic Archives, 33, 36, 37, 65 (top), 81, 97 (bottom),100, 101 (top), 117 (bottom), 120 (bottom), 124 (top), 130, 131, 132, 148, 149 (top), 151 (bottom), 164, 178 (center & bottom); National Park Service, 169, 170 (top); Historical Museum of Southern Florida, 10 (bottom), 73 (top); Hillsborough River State Park, 77 (top right); Library of Congress, 56 (bottom); U.S. Navy, 137 (bottom); War Department, 136 (top); and illustrations from Dover Publishing, 6 (top), 8 (top right), 12 (bottom), 86 (top left), 96 (top), 97 (top), 98 (top), 99, 101 (bottom).

Library of Congress Control Number: 2011922122

Designed by Stephanie Daugherty
Type set in Trajan Pro/Humanst521 BT
ISBN: 978-0-7643-3714-7
Printed in China

Schiffer Publishing Ltd.
4880 Lower Valley Road
Atglen, PA 19310
Phone: (610) 593-1777; Fax: (610) 593-2002
E-mail: Info@schifferbooks.com

In Europe, Schiffer books are distributed by
Bushwood Books
6 Marksbury Ave.
Kew Gardens
Surrey TW9 4JF England
Phone: 44 (0) 20 8392 8585; Fax: 44 (0) 20 8392 9876
E-mail: info@bushwoodbooks.co.uk
Website: www.bushwoodbooks.co.uk

CONTENTS

PREFACE

Throughout history, mankind has demonstrated the need to defend itself against aggressors and predators — from the most basic defenses of the earliest civilizations to the high-tech fortifications of the modern world.

Military battles and involvements, as well as forts and military camps, have been part of the scene in Florida since the earliest times. History seems to place them into seven categories:

- Indian skirmishes from prehistoric times
- Battles and forts from the Early Colonial Period
- Seminole Indian battles and forts
- Civil War battles and forts
- Training camps during World War I
- Military bases during World War II
- Military operations of modern times

Throughout much of Florida's history, the state's extensive waterways have challenged the defensive capabilities of various nations (Spain, France, and England) seeking to colonize the state. Leaders of each successive nation arriving here have asserted their claims by constructing fortifications to protect potential waterfront entry points. Most forts constructed of highly perishable materials such as wood have not survived, in contrast with the more durable brick and stone structures. Historical markers commemorate many of the battlegrounds and forts that have perished. Other forts still stand; many of them have been preserved or restored.

Florida at War: Forts and Battles describes the battles, forts and other topics that preserve and honor the heritage of Florida's bitter conflicts from prehistoric Indian skirmishes to wars of modern times.

1

FLORIDA'S MILITARY HISTORY

Florida's first people, called Native Americans, made their way to the region roughly 12,000 years ago. They migrated from place to place as they searched for food. Some of the people hunted animals on the land, others caught fish, and still others collected berries and fruit that grew naturally. The area that would eventually become Florida was a lot different 12,000 years ago than it is today. The weather was cooler and drier. There were large prehistoric animals, such as mastodons, mammoths, giant ground sloths, as well as many smaller animals, deer, raccoons, snakes, and turtles.

Thousands of years later the descendants of the first people began to settle down a little more. New sources of food had appeared, such as frogs, squirrels, aquatic birds, and alligators. By 3,000 years ago there was more moisture in the air, temperatures began to rise, and small villages began to appear. It wasn't long before there were chiefs who ruled good-sized villages or towns; beans, corn, and squash were being grown in community gardens in some parts of what would become Florida. Burial mounds were created, as was pottery and woven baskets.

THE FLORIDA NATIVES

Many different Native American people lived in what would eventually become Florida. Some of the major groups were the Calusa Indians in the southwest area, the Tequesta in the southeast area, the Timucua in the northeast area, and the Apalachee in the northwest area. There were also many smaller groups scattered on the Florida peninsula.

Although all these different peoples spoke unique languages and often clashed with one another, their lifestyles and customs were similar. Chieftains and religious leaders ruled many of the early Native American tribes. Several of the villages were arranged around a chieftain's house and council buildings, in which meetings took place. Many of the houses were made from small branches woven together and then covered with mud and clay. The roofs of these houses were thatched with palm fronds.

A Timucua Indian Village. When Europeans first arrived in North America in the early 1500s, people had been living for thousands of years in the area that would become Florida. Some of the major groups were the Timucua Indians in the northeast area, the Apalachee Indians in the northwest, the Tequesta in the southeast, and the Calusa in the southwest. There were many more smaller Indian tribes.

Many of the early Indian tribes were very hostile to the Europeans who landed on their shores. Warfare was a common occurrence between the Indians and the visiting Europeans.

PONCE DE LEON CLAIMS FLORIDA

Spanish explorers were the first Europeans to make contact with Florida's Native Americans. A fleet sailing from Puerto Rico under Juan Ponce de Leon landed in Florida in 1513. Ponce de Leon named the peninsula Florida. Ponce de Leon stayed in the area only five days, but in that short time he planted the Spanish flag and took possession of the land in the name of the King of Spain. In 1521, Ponce de Leon returned to Florida. This time he sailed along the

Ponce de Leon Discovers Florida. Spanish explorer Juan Ponce de Leon discovered Florida in 1513. He returned in 1521 to establish a colony and met hostile Calusa Indians in southwest Florida which resulted in his death.

lower southwestern coast and landed in the Port Charlotte area. There he tried to establish a settlement for Spain with colonists, cattle, and seeds that he had brought with him. Soon, though, the Calusa Indians had attacked the little settlement. Ponce de Leon was wounded, but escaped with some of the people from the settlement. They reached Cuba safely, however, Ponce de Leon died within a few days.

Spanish and French Explorers Invade Florida

Ponce de Leon believed Florida was one big island. The expeditions of Spanish explorers Panfilo Narvaez in 1528, Hernando de Soto in 1539, and others revealed that it was only a finger of land from the continent of North America. The Spaniards laid claim to all of it—to the whole of North America in fact. They explored much of Florida, but did not find what they really wanted — gold and silver.

While Spain was bringing great wealth from its many colonies in North and South America, other countries had been enviously waiting for their own chance. French Protestants, called Huguenots, were anxious to find a place in the New World where they could worship freely. In 1562, French leader Jean Ribault laid claim to the land near the St. Johns River for France. Two years after the Ribault expedition, explorer Rene Laudonniere returned to Florida with three ships and a crowd of Huguenots for settlement. The French built Fort Caroline five miles from the mouth of the St. Johns River.

Spain, meanwhile, was horrified that Protestants were attempting to take away her rights in Florida. She hurriedly sent one of her great leaders, conquistador Pedro Menendez, to drive the intruders out and restore the land to Spanish control.

Menendez and his soldiers attacked Fort Caroline and massacred the French colonists. South of the destroyed French settlement, Menendez founded St. Augustine in 1565, which became the first permanent European settlement in what is today the United States. France did not attempt another permanent settlement in Florida again until the late 1600s, and then it chose the upper Gulf Coast.

Trouble with England

Though France was no longer a threat in Florida, Spain's problems there were far from over. England loomed as the next danger. In 1586, English pirate Sir Frances Drake burned and looted St. Augustine. Then England successfully settled Jamestown, Virginia in 1607, Charleston, South Carolina in 1670, and Savannah, Georgia, in 1733.

Indians Resisting Spanish Invasions. The coming of the Spanish explorers into the Florida territory was a direct threat to the Indians. Many battles occurred between Spanish conquistadors and Florida's Native Indians. Shown are the Calusa Indians in southwest Florida fighting savagely against a Spanish invasion.

DeSoto's Landing. In 1539 Spanish explorer, Hernando DeSoto and 620 Spaniards landed on Florida's west coast. The Native Indians were no better pleased to see DeSoto's Spanish army than they had been to see earlier explorers Ponce de Leon or Panfilo Narvaez expeditions, and there was one fight after another.

DeSoto Explores Florida. Hernando DeSoto's search took him deep into the swamps and forests of Florida. DeSoto's troops encountered many hostile Indians and several bloody battles occurred.

DeSoto National Memorial. Located four miles west of Bradenton, among the lush green background of Gumbo Limbo trees and the Mangrove swamp, the DeSoto National Memorial commemorates the 1539 landing of Spanish conquistador Hernando DeSoto and the Europeans' first extensive and organized exploration of what is now the southern United States.

Indians Greeted the French. In 1562 the Timucua Indians in northeast Florida welcomed French explorer Jean Ribault. Two years later the Indians helped French explorer Rene de Laudonniere and his soldiers build Fort Caroline in northeast Florida.

Timucua Indian Warriors. A ceremony prior to going on the warpath against an enemy Indian tribe. The Timucua Indians, in northeast Florida, were warlike and well organized military.

Marching Off to Another War. Chief Holata Outina, in the center of the orderly ranks, marching his Timucua Indian warriors on a military expedition. The Indians often wore animal heads and tails to make them ferocious in battle. Many of the Indians carried heavy clubs to be used in close combat, and their fingernails were filed to sharp points to facilitate the gouging of the enemies' foreheads in order to blind them with the flow of blood. Engraving from DeBry, 1591, after LeMoyne, 1564.

Potano-Outina Battle. With the help of French soldiers, Timucua Indian Chief, Outina, gains a victory over an enemy Indian tribe, led by Potano. Engraving from DeBry, 1591, after LeMoyne, 1564.

Menendez Arrives to Destroy Fort Caroline. The Timucua Indians gave Spanish conquistador Pedro Menendez and his soldiers information about the location of the French Fort Caroline.

Menendez Destroys Fort Caroline. In 1565, Spanish commander, Pedro Menendez, and his army destroyed Fort Caroline and most of its defenders.

Matanzas Inlet Massacre. Historical rendition of Spanish conquistador Pedro Menendez and his army of soldiers wiping out the French Huguenots who originally settled in northeast Florida in 1562. Here in 1565 Mendez killed over 200 French at Matanzas Inlet.

The Founding of St. Augustine. On September 8, 1565, Spanish explorer Pedro Menendez established the town of St. Augustine. In quick order Menendez and his men made friends with the Timucua Indians, moved into the "great house" of their village, and built a moated fortification.

Spanish Explorers Land in South Florida. Spanish soldiers arrived at the Tequesta Indian village on the north bank of the Miami River. This postcard of a painting by Ken Hughs shows an artist's reconstruction of the first recorded European contact (1567) in the Greater Miami area, commissioned by the Historical Museum of Southern Florida.

The government of Spain eyed these growing settlements with considerable worry, but did not try to stop them. Rather, Spain elected to strengthen its position in Florida. Part of its strategy was to convert Florida's Indians to Christianity and to convince them to side with Spain against the British. In 1672, Spain began construction of Castillo de San Marcos, an enormous coquina stone fort that still stands in St. Augustine, which gave them a military base with which to counter attacks from the British.

Under the British Flag (1763-1783)

England wanted Florida in order to round out the colonies on the eastern seaboard. Spain was firmly entrenched. In the war known as the French and Indian War, lasting from 1754 to 1763, Spain took part with France against England. At the end of the war Spain was forced to give up Florida to the English to regain Cuba.

One of the first acts of government by the English was to divide the colony into East and West Florida. East Florida lay between the Atlantic Ocean and the Apalachicola River. West Florida extended from the Apalachicola to the Mississippi River.

To encourage the settlement of the new territories, the English government gave generous land grants to officers and soldiers who had served in the war. Good public roads were made; indigo, sugar cane, and fruits were cultivated; and lumber was shipped — the Floridas prospered as they had never done before.

Spain Again (1783-1821)

Florida remained under British rule throughout the Revolutionary War, giving refuge to many English sympathizers from Georgia and South Carolina. When the war ended in 1783 and the American colonies became independent states, England ceded East and West Florida back to Spain in exchange for the Bahama Islands.

After most of the English left Florida to seek homes in England, Nova Scotia, Jamaica, or the Bahamas, the Spanish did not find it easy to get new colonists in place of the English. Some estates were now unoccupied, and settlements were abandoned. The few people at St. Augustine hardly dared go beyond the protection of the guns of the fort; the Indians now began to give trouble in various ways.

War of 1812

During the early 1800s, the British were trying to regain control of Florida. This desire became stronger in 1812, when the United States and Britain went to war. Britain wanted to make Florida a base from which to attack Americans.

In 1813, the British took control of Pensacola. From here they attacked American forts and settlements in the southeastern United States. The United States sent Andrew Jackson with a small army to drive the British army out of the region. After a hard bitter struggle the war came to an end on March 27, 1814.

The U.S. Acquires Florida

Spain was unable to control the Indians and rule her territory. Finally, after much discussion, a treaty was signed in which Spain agreed to transfer Florida to the United States for the sum of five million dollars, and the payment of certain claims. The exchange of flags took place on July 10, 1821, at St. Augustine (capital of East Florida), and on July 17, 1821, at Pensacola (capital of West Florida). After more than 300 years of Spanish and British rule, Florida became part of the United States.

In 1822, the United States made Florida a Territory. It then began to prepare Florida for statehood.

Change of Flags. The Castillo de San Marcos and Florida came into American hands through a treaty signed with Spain in 1821. On July 10th, the Spanish Flag came down for the last time, and the twenty-three starred flag of the United States rose over the old embattlements.

Seminole Wars

The three Seminole Indian wars were brought on by U.S. territorial expansion, native factions resisting the U.S. policy of removal, and slavery. There was a constant turmoil on the Florida border. Slaves seeking freedom slipped across from Georgia and Alabama. Parties of slave catchers roved in Spanish North Florida. The Spanish government could not maintain order.

During the Seminole Wars of 1817-1818 (First Seminole War) and 1835-1842 (Second Seminole War), Florida became saturated with forts, camps, stockades, and blockhouses of all descriptions. During this period more than eighty forts were in use throughout Florida.

Seminole Indians Resisted Removal From Florida. As Florida expanded, the Native Seminole Indians resisted the U.S. policy of removal and slavery. There was constant turmoil throughout the state. During the 1800s there were three wars between the Seminole Indians and the U.S. Army.

Florida Becomes A State

In 1838, Floridians held a convention for the purpose of writing a constitution or a set of laws by which the state would be governed. Fifty-six people from all parts of the territory took part in this convention. Florida voters approved the constitution in 1839 and six years later Florida became the twenty-seventh state in the United States.

Civil War

The Civil War was a period of internal conflict for the United States. In 1861 Florida seceded from the Union and joined the newly formed country, the Confederate States of America. Also in 1861, the Civil War began between the United States of America and the Confederate States of America. The war between the North and South lasted four long years, 1861-1865. It was the most tragic war in American history. More Americans died in the War Between the States than in all wars of the United States combined, until the Vietnam War.

Civil War.
In 1861 the Civil War began between the United States of America and the Confederate States of America, the thirteen southern states, including Florida. It was the most tragic war in American history. Florida provided an estimated 15,000 troops and significant amounts of supplies to the Confederacy.

World War II. Between 1942 and 1945, Florida served as a training ground for all branches of the military service. Hotels were converted to barracks, hospitals, and training schools. Military bases were located throughout the state.

Spanish-American War

At the end of the nineteenth century, America became involved in a short war. The Spanish-American War began in 1898 and lasted only 120 days. Shortly after the sinking of the battleship *U.S.S. Maine* in Cuba, the United States declared war on Spain. Florida immediately became the grounds of military activity: Key West became an important naval base; military training camps were established in Fernandina, Jacksonville, Lakeland, Miami, and Tampa; and Tampa became the principal port of embarkation to Cuba. Colonel Theodore Roosevelt and his Rough Riders were to go to Cuba to put an end to the fighting, but the fighting was over in three months.

World War I

During World War I (1917-1919), Florida was particularly suited to the training of pilots because of its year-round good weather; the state quickly took a lead in aviation. In this war Florida people more than did their part, both at homes and on the fighting fronts. Over 42,000 Floridians served in this war.

Florida During World War II

World War II brought the Great Depression to an end. It also brought a new surge of people and energy to the Sunshine State. Florida served as a training ground for all branches of the military service. The state was ideal for training because of its year-round good weather and flat terrain. It was particularly useful for pilot training. By the war's end in 1945, Florida had forty military bases.

Tourism was disrupted during the war. Hotels were converted to barracks, hospitals, and training schools; beaches were patrolled by military aircraft, the Civil Air patrol, cavalry, blimps, and automobiles; and most of the coast-watching was designed to spot German submarines, which occasionally torpedoed transport ships within sight of the coast early in the war.

Korean Conflict

In 1950, the Communists from North Korea invaded South Korea. President Harry Truman asked for the United Nations to protect South Korea, which it did. The United States supplied the majority of the troops. The war lasted until 1953. During this conflict 972 men of the Florida National Guard were called to active duty. In addition to these, 27,823 Floridians were drafted and 84,257 voluntarily enlisted. More than 500 Floridians died or were killed in action. The Korean conflict was fought under presidential powers and was not declared a war.

Vietnam War

After World War II, Vietnam was divided into North and South sections. To help stop the spread of communism, U.S. Presidents Eisenhower and Kennedy sent military advisors to aid South Vietnam. Under President Lyndon B. Johnson almost 500,000 American personnel were sent to combat in Vietnam. President Richard M. Nixon started reducing the number of military personnel and by 1972 only air bombardment by Americans aided South Vietnam. The United States withdrew from Vietnam in 1973. Over 186,000 Floridians fought in the Vietnam conflict.

Iraq and Afghanistan

Many Florida military personnel have been involved in protecting the freedom we have in America by participating in wars in Iraq (1991 and since 2003) and Afghanistan (since 2001).

2

Colonial Period: Battles and Forts

Under Spain, France, or England, in their early settlements, the first thing done in all instances was to build a fort to be used as a rallying point for colonists in times of stress and danger, a dwelling place for troops, a supply depot, and a defense against hostile forces.

Early Florida forts include France's Fort Caroline, built in 1564 near the mouth of the St. Johns River; the Spanish Castillo de San Marcos, built in 1672-1695 in St. Augustine; the small Spanish Fort Matanzas built in 1740-1742 on an island near the Matanzas Inlet; the stone fort at St. Marks, which replaced a series of wooden stockades; several forts at Pensacola including Fort George and Fort San Carlos; and Fort Mose (originally called Fort Moosa), which was built by Negro refugees from the British Crown colonies. Most of these forts changed hands several times until Florida became a U.S. territory. In addition to major military centers, many small outposts stretched across North Florida and along the coasts.

Early colonial forts were built to protect and defend the established forces against any and all aggressors. Along waterways these early fortifications occupied commanding positions opposite harbors, bays, or ship channels and would face any entering or passing vessel. However, the limited effective range of the cannon in this time period allowed many vessels to pass within sight of the fortifications with complete safety.

The early forts, all made of wood, suffered numerous and varied fates. They were burnt by Sir Francis Drake in 1586, looted by buccaneer Captain John Davis in 1665, and often toppled into the sea due to destructive sea corrosion. St. Augustine underwent many changes before the massive coquina rock fort was built. There were at least nine wooden forts built, one after another, until 1672 when construction started on the permanent fort.

Permanent forts were often massive brick or stone (coquina rock) structures. Cannons were mounted behind low parapets facing the sea. Wide stairways led to elevated vantage points where riflemen were protected by thick walls. Castillo de San Marcos, the great coquina fort in St. Augustine, remains to this day the most perfect example of Spanish military architecture in North America. The present structure was completed in 1695; was under construction for twenty-three years; and cost more than 138,000 pesos ($218,630).

Other forts, built by the U.S. Government, were uniform and conform to others built throughout the United States early during the nineteenth century. These forts were built of massive, common brick, which was the predominate construction material at that time. The interiors were galleried with tunnels with narrow ports for observation and riflemen usage while offering excellent protection. These openings were usually "V" shaped with the wide side, or opening, inward, closing to a smaller opening on the exterior surface. All galleries were roofed with brick; barrel arches and openings were surmounted with brick arches. The area above the galleries and behind parapets was used as a sand fill.

The designs of these old fortifications show that the manner of defense intended riflemen to stand in the space behind the breastworks and do battle with the opposing aggressors. Ports permit cannons to fire down the length of the dry moats and defenders to fire through the port openings during the final stages of battle.

Many of the early Florida inland forts were established to protect camps, stores, and lines of communication for the military forces active in Florida during the Colonial Period. These forts, many of them temporary forts, outposts, and fortified barracks with makeshift walls, did little more than keep out the weather. Needless to say, all wooden structures were either destroyed by fire or gave way to decay. They are buried relics of a forgotten past.

When the United States acquired Florida, the U.S. Army assumed control of the existing forts. However, they did very little to improve most of them and several were abandoned. The American defense strategy was different than that of their colonial counterparts, as the United States recognized that

Florida's Coastal Forts. Fortifications were a common feature of early Florida settlements. The rivalry of the European powers, Spain, France, and England, made such fortifications necessary.

it was impossible to defend her entire coastline and instead concentrated on building forts to protect important naval bases and to deny invaders important harbors and anchorages.

When Pensacola was selected as the site of the major U.S. Navy base (Navy Yard) on the Gulf of Mexico, it also became the site of the most intensive fortification effort in Florida. Fort Pickens, located on Santa Rosa Island at the mouth of Pensacola Bay, was begun in 1829. On the opposite side of the channel from Fort Pickens, Fort McRee was built. The Army used part of Fort San Carlos, and added Fort Barrancas and the Advanced Redoubt.

To defend the other major naval base in Florida, at Key West, the Army built Fort Zachary Taylor and started two smaller forts called the Martello Towers. Construction on the Towers stopped at the conclusion of the Civil War before either tower was completed. The other locations fortified before the Civil War were Fernandina (Fort Clinch) and Dry Tortugas, west of Key West (Fort Jefferson).

The forts of this period were brick or stone closed structures, usually in a regular geometric shape. At the corners were prominent bastions from which cross-fires could be established to defend the walls from infantry attacks. The forts were designed with tiers of cannons and usually surrounded by dry moats.

Fort Barrancas. Built to guard the head of the pass into Pensacola Bay, the fort also protected the Pensacola Navy Yard against a landward attack.

Fort Barrancas

Erected by the U.S. between 1839 and 1844, Fort Barrancas' purpose was to protect the harbor during the tumultuous battles of Pensacola's illustrious past. Barranca is a Spanish word for a bluff. This strategic coastal site was the focal point for many of Pensacola's battles during its various military occupations. The fort was designed to defend Pensacola harbor with a cross fire from Santa Rosa Island where Fort Pickens had been erected in the sand dunes a few years earlier.

The 300 by 300 foot triangular shaped brick fort faces south with a sally port entrance on the north and dry moats on the northeast and northwest sides. Inner works and moats are flanked by a series of vaulted casements and galleries with embrasures opening into the moat. The interior has heavy wood plank doors with strap hinges. The parade ground has numerous semicircular granite gun mounts and iron tracks in place. There is also a round brick well and a brick tunnel that leads to the adjoining Fort San Carlos, which was built between 1781 and 1790 on the approximate site of two earlier wooden forts, one constructed by d'Arriola in 1698, the other by the British about 1771. The brickwork is exceptionally well crafted, composed of thin, long, locally handmade, Roman-style bricks. The main walls are twenty feet high and four feet thick, providing defense against both ships and infantry. The center of the fort held a shot furnace for heating cannonballs. Though an earthen slope hid the fort from land-based artillery, masonry forts were only effective against ships. An army conducting a siege could capture a fort in two weeks.

Cabbage Swamp Battle

The Battle of Cabbage Swamp was fought near Fort McIntosh, off of the St. Marys River, in June 1778 when a force of three hundred Americans attacked British soldiers under Colonel Thomas Brown.

Fort Carlos

This fort was established by the Spanish prior to 1763 in present day Fernandina Beach.

Carlos Blockhouse

This Spanish blockhouse was located on the Bahamas Channel near Key Biscayne (Miami).

Fort Barrancas and Fort San Carlos. Fort Barrancas is a Pensacola fortification still standing to remind visitors of the area's turbulent history under five flags. Built between 1839 and 1844, Fort Barrancas was located on a bluff above and behind Fort San Carlos, a Spanish fort built in 1797.

Pensacola Fort Ruins.
The Advanced Redoubt was built to assist Fort Barrancas (700 yards south) in protecting Pensacola Navy Yard from overland assault. Fort Pickens, Fort McRee, Fort Barrancas, and the Advanced Redoubt created an interlocking system of defense. This illustration is a 1903 postcard view of the Redoubt.

Advanced Redoubt.
A contemporary view of the Advanced Redoubt for Fort Barrancas.

Fort Caroline

In the mid-sixteenth century, France was a vigorous, expansionist nation emerging from feudalism and dreaming of empire. Spain, the world's leading power, already had a foothold in the Americas, and France wanted a share of the riches Spain was gaining through trade and plunder. France's first attempt to stake a permanent claim in North America was Fort Caroline, a settlement near the mouth of the St. Johns River in Florida.

Initially the settlement was to be a commercial venture, but religious conflict in France broadened the goals. The growing persecution of French Protestants (Huguenots) led their most powerful member, Admiral Gaspard de Coligny, to propose to the crown that the colony also be a refuge for Huguenots. An exploratory expedition commanded by Jean Ribault left France in February 1562. After erecting a monument at the River of May (now St. Johns River), Ribault headed north, left a small garrison at Charlesfort near Port Royal Sound, and sailed home. Within months the situation of his men became desperate, and they returned to France.

Laudonniere Builds Fort Caroline

Coligny urged another attempt in April 1564 planning for a permanent settlement of 110 sailors, 120 soldiers, and seventy artisans and servants. Led by Rene Laudonniere, who had accompanied Ribault on his previous expedition, the colonists first touched at the River of May on June 22. With help from the Timucua Indians, under Chief Saturiwa, they began building a village and Fort Caroline on the river's south bank.

Fort Caroline contained a guardhouse, a granary, an arms magazine, storehouses, and a well. A kitchen was built outside the fort in order to avoid the risk of fire.

Good relations with the Indians eventually soured and by the following spring the colonists were close to starvation. Mutinous parties sailed off to make their own fortune and some were eventually captured by the Spanish, revealing the presence of the French colony. The remaining colonists, having failed to discover silver or gold, were about to leave Florida in August 1565, when Ribault arrived with a relief expedition of supplies and 600 soldiers and settlers, including more women and some children.

French Land and Build Fort Caroline. Captain Rene de Laudonniere, on June 22, 1564, arrived in New France (Florida) with his three ships and some 200 French Huguenot (Protestant) noblemen, soldiers, and artisans, landing along the River of May (St. Johns River). The French found a site (St. Johns Bluff) for their settlement on June 30. Protected by a bluff commanding a river view, the spot offered fertile land, potable water, woodland fruits and building materials, and an abundance of fish. The French soldiers thought the ground defensible and its closeness to the sea afforded access for ships. Above all, the Timucua Indians seemed friendly and willing to help them in their new world.

Fort Caroline National Memorial. This earth and wood fort model memorializes the French attempt at permanent colonization in what became the United States. This model fort is located in the Timucuan Ecological and Historical Preserve just east of Jacksonville.

Timucua Indians Help Build Fort Caroline. Timucua Chief Saturiwa's men crafted a shelter, similar to the one shown, so Saturiwa could sit and watch the colonists build their settlement. When the French requested help, Saturiwa sent eighty of his strongest men. The natives helped dig Fort Caroline's moat; they gathered palmetto leaves, weaving a thatch to cover the colonists' houses. The Timucua Indians gave of their bounty — gold and silver jewelry, pearls, animal hides, and medicinal plants. In return, Saturiwa sought a war alliance to help his people. When the alliance never materialized, Timucua Indian assistance dwindled.

Spain Destroys the French Settlement

Fort Caroline's very existence mocked Spain's claim to Florida and threatened the passage of the Spanish treasure fleets that followed the Gulf Stream and swung close inshore. Spain responded by sending out an expedition both to settle Florida and to drive out the French.

On learning of Ribault's departure for Florida, Philip II of Spain sent Admiral Pedro Menendez to dislodge the French. Initially rebuffed off the coast, Menendez established a base to the south at San Augustine. Ribault sailed down the coast seeking to attack the Spanish, but his ships were scattered by a hurricane and beached far to the south. Seizing the opportunity, Menendez marched north with 500 soldiers to attack Fort Caroline. Early in the morning of September 20, his troops massacred 140 settlers, sparing only about sixty women and children. About fifty others, including Laudonniere, escaped and sailed for France. Menendez next marched south and found the shipwrecked Frenchmen, Ribault among them. They threw themselves on his mercy, but to Menendez they were heretics and enemies of his king. At a place later named Matanzas ("slaughter") he put to the sword about 350 men — all but those professing to be Catholics, and a few musicians.

Fort Caroline was kept as a fort for several years by the Spanish, who changed the name of the fort and the river to San Mateo.

Fort Caroline. The French built Fort Caroline near the mouth of the St. Johns River. The fort was destroyed September 20, 1565, when the French were massacred by Spanish conquistadors who had been sent to reclaim the area for Spain.

Castillo de San Marcos. This fort was built by the Spaniards in the years following 1672. It is now the oldest existing fortification in America. Over it have flown the flags of Spain, Great Britain, the Confederacy, and the United States. The Castillo took twenty-three years to build and cost more than 138,000 pesos ($218,630). The design of the fort is "stellar." It has a square central courtyard with a series of storage rooms around it with diamond-shaped bastions at each corner.

Castillo de San Marcos

Fifty years after making discovery in 1513, Spain still had neglected to establish a colony in Florida. When the French built Fort Caroline near the mouth of the St. Johns River on Spanish-claimed territory, it touched off the first armed conflict between European powers in North America. More importantly, though, while ejecting the French from Fort Caroline and Florida and attempting to protect her treasure-laden galleons sailing along the coasts of Florida from the New World to the Old, Spain founded St. Augustine, about thirty-five miles south of the French colony.

The northernmost military outpost in Spain's vast colonial empire, St. Augustine, was the first permanent European settlement on the continent, and the political, military, and religious capital of Florida. Since the mid-1500s, St. Augustine had been guarded by a series of wooden fortifications that always succumbed to weak construction and the effects of salt, wind, rot, and fire.

Sir Francis Drake's raid upon St. Augustine in 1586 was a sign of the times — and of England's determination to destroy the Spanish monopoly in the New World. No Spanish ship or settlement was safe. As a result, Spain tightened the convoys and built massive forts at key harbors in the Caribbean.

St. Augustine, no wealthy seaport, had little more than palisade earthworks. Its real protection was the Franciscan priests, patiently making converts among the Indians. It was realized that natives friendly to Spain would be unfriendly to Spain's enemies, but in Virginia, the English gained a foothold on the Spanish-claimed continent. English traders, turning Indian enemies into allies, crumbled the Spanish defense. English pirate Robert Searles sacked St. Augustine in 1668. Concerned about the security of the northern gateway to their empire, Spanish officials persuaded Mariana, the queen regent, to approve allocations to build the tenth, and final, fortification in St. Augustine.

In 1669, Queen Mariana of Spain appointed Sergeant Major Manuel de Cendoya to be the new governor of Florida. Mariana charged Cendoya with the assignment of seeing that an "adequate fortification" was constructed in St. Augustine. This fort was needed for protection from pirate attacks and to also protect Spanish territory from encroachment by the English.

Don Manuel de Cendoya (Governor of Florida, 1669-1673) arrived in St. Augustine on July 6, 1671, with his family, soldiers, master masons, master stonecutters, master lime burners, and money to pay soldiers and workers to build the fort. Cendoya was ready to assume his duties as Governor and Captain General of Florida. Six days later he gave the order to begin construction of the new fort using a local stone called "coquina" — tiny calcified shells forged over many millennia into shell rock.

Skilled stonecutters chopped blocks of coquina rock out of pits from nearby Anastasia Island. Workers loaded the large blocks onto wagons. Oxen pulled the wagons to the wharf. There Timucua Indians, slaves, and convicts hauled the blocks onto rafts that ferried them across the Matanzas River to the Castillo building site. Meanwhile, other workers dumped oyster shells into hot kilns, or ovens. The heated shells changed into lime, which was used for mortar to hold the coquina blocks together for the fort's walls.

During this same time, Ignacio Daza, the engineer assigned to this project by the Queen Regent, arrived in St. Augustine from Cuba and began designing the layout of the new stone fort, which would be a nearly square central hollow body with a series of storage rooms around a central courtyard with diamond-shaped bastions at each corner, plus a triangular-shaped ravelin opposite the sally port.

Groundbreaking for The Castillo

The site was selected by Governor Cendoya, treasury officials, sergeants major and captains, and all of the expert and skilled men in town. All finally agreed on a location north of the present wooden fort; the site would make it closer to the harbor entrance, prevent the entry of invading enemy vessels, and give better protection from storm flooding.

On October 2, 1672, workers and officials gathered for the ground breaking of the new fort, Castillo de San Marcos. Digging out the area where the fort would sit was a difficult task due to its closeness to the water. Each high tide, water would fill in the area they had dug and when the tide went out, digging would start again.

Building the Fort

Usually about 150 men at a time were working on the fort. These included Native Americans (the Apalachee, Timucua, and Guale Indians) and blacks. White artisans, (stonecutters, overseers, blacksmiths, teamsters, quarrymen, lime burners and boatmen), worked hard with convict laborers (both Spanish and captured Englishmen). All was done under the watchful eyes of Master Mason Lorenzo LaJones.

The foundation of the fort began taking shape, but neither Cendoya nor Daza would live to see its completion. Many of the laborers became ill so Cendoya began doing construction on the fort himself, putting in many long hard hours, day after day. He too became ill, possibly a victim of the same illness the laborers had and/or from overwork. On March 8, 1673, Cendoya died and less than two weeks later

Moat and Towers. The moat and towers of the massive Castillo de San Marcos helped it withstand many assaults.

Daza followed Cendoya in death. At the time of their death, the two seaward bastions and the curtain of the Castillo de San Marcos had been raised to a height of eleven feet. Other governors, engineers, masons, and stonecutters would come and go before the fort would be completed.

Design of the Fort

Castillo de San Marcos has four nearly equal bastions known as San Agustin, San Carlos, San Pablo, and San Pedro, and four connecting walls called curtains. On three of the bastions are sentry towers, while on that to the northeast stands a high watchtower with a commanding view of both the land and water.

The Castillo's walls stood thirty-three feet above the moat. The north, south, and west walls ranged in thickness from fourteen feet at the base to nine feet at the top. The east wall, facing the Matanzas Bay, ranged in thickness from nineteen feet at the base to eleven feet at the top. Within the fort are living quarters for the garrison, guard rooms, storerooms, a chapel, powder magazine and prisons. Beautifully arched casements and interesting cornices testify to the workmanship and imagination of the Spanish builders.

The covering over the space between the inner and outer walls is called the terreplein. That's where the guns were mounted. Around the outer edge of the terreplein is a wall three feet thick and six feet high known as the parapet. The ascent to the terreplein is an incline plane known as the ramp, now converted to steps. The plaza or inner court is 100 feet square and the casemates, with one or two exceptions, open into it. There are twenty-six casemates, five dungeons, and one magazine. The only entrance to the fort is through the Sally Port in the middle of the south curtain.

The chapel, without which no Spanish fort is complete, is directly opposite the Sally Port. Niches in the walls supported two fonts for holy water and the location of the altar place is still discernible. It is said that the doors at both sides of the chapel originally had iron bars behind which condemned prisoners stood to hear Mass.

The majority of the casemates or rooms open on the inner court and are generally alike with heavy doors, barred windows, and dim light filtering through narrow slits in the 8-foot curtains, high up near the arched ceilings.

The two casemates at the right of the entrance were guard rooms and contain fireplaces. Leading off from the inner of these rooms is a large dungeon that was used as the prison. The casemate at the left of the entrance was the Commander's quarters, while the other officers used the two rooms leading off from that.

For maximum security, the fort was surrounded by a moat and had only one entrance — located on the town side so that the inhabitants could take refuge in the fort at the first hint of danger.

The fort walls were covered with a smooth, gleaming white coat of lime plaster made from burned oyster shells to waterproof and protect the masonry. The sentry boxes were emblazoned with red paint.

On August 31, 1695, the fortress was completed and ready to be used to defend St. Augustine in the name of Spain, but, although the Castillo was the most important fortification in Colonial Florida, it was by no means the only defense. Earthworks and palisades extended from the fort to enclose the little town of St. Augustine, an area of less than a square mile. Far to the south, west,

Fort Sally Port. The Sally Port is the only entrance and exit to the Castillo de San Marcos.

Castillo Stairs. The stairs were originally a smooth ramp to pull cannons up to the gundeck. The steps were added in the mid-1750s to replace the ramp.

and north were military outposts. Sixteen miles to the south was the strongest of these, Fort Matanzas, which guarded the lower entrance to St. Augustine harbor. Two miles north of the city, Fort Mose was built and garrisoned by former slaves in 1738 and rebuilt in 1752.

British Attacks

The fort's construction was so solid that it withstood heavy and prolonged sieges. In 1702, South Carolina's Governor James Moore with 500 men seized St. Augustine and unsuccessfully besieged the fort for fifty days. Before Moore left, he set fire to the town. Moore also destroyed the Spanish missions of Florida and carried off 1,400 Indians as slaves.

In 1728, British troops from South Carolina marched to St. Augustine. They turned back at the sight of the Spanish cannons in the stone walls of the Castillo.

In 1740, with an attack force of 900 men and a fleet of thirteen vessels, James Oglethorpe,

British Occupation.
The English held the Castillo from 1763, when Florida was ceded to them, until 1783, when Spain regained possession. During the British ownership, the fort was called Fort St. Mark and used as a base from which to launch attacks against Georgia and South Carolina. Fort St. Mark was also used as a British prison. The Castillo de San Marcos was declared a National Monument in 1924. It is run by the National Park Service and is one of Florida's most important historic monuments.

Fort Location West of the Matanzas River. The thickest part of the fort's walls is forty feet. The structure covers five acres. There are inner and outer barriers, and the draw bridge and moat.

Coquina Walls. Cannons battering the coquina walls of the Castillo had no effect. Cannonballs simply bounced off or got stuck in the soft rock without breaking it.

the founder of Georgia, attacked St. Augustine. While the British fleet blockaded the harbor to starve the Spaniards, English gunners shelled the town and fort. The fort suffered only slight damage. After twenty-seven days, Oglethorpe gave up and went back to Georgia.

In 1763, however, the English finally secured Florida by terms of a treaty.

The Castillo Becomes Fort Marion

Eventually the Castillo and Florida came into American hands through a treaty signed in 1821. On July 10th, the Spanish flag came down for the last time, and the twenty-three starred flag of the United States rose over the old embattlements. In 1824 Congress ordered the name of the Castillo changed to Fort Marion. This was to honor General Francis Marion of South Carolina, known as the famous "Swamp Fox" of the Revolutionary War.

Original Name Restored

In 1900, after the Spanish-American War, Fort Marion was decommissioned as an active military base. In 1924, it was designated a National Monument by Presidential Proclamation. The National Park Service assumed administration in 1935, and in 1942 Congress restored the fort's original Spanish name, Castillo de San Marcos, to this nation's oldest masonry fortification.

Cannon-ball Shooting Gun. This Cannon-ball shooting gun at the Castillo de San Marcos still points out to sea.

Cantonment Clinch

Established in 1823 at Bayou Chico, about three miles west of Pensacola, the post was named for Colonel (later General) Duncan Lamont Clinch. It consisted of ten large log-built houses, each one designed to accommodate a company of troops.

Creek Indian Warriors

Hounded by soldiers in Georgia and constantly in danger of being captured and made slaves, an angry band of Creek Indians came to Florida in 1750, led by Chief Seecoffee (Cowkeeper), a bloodthirsty warrior who was proud of the eighty-six Spanish soldiers he had killed. The Indians settled on the Alachua prairie, the present day Payne's Prairie south of Gainesville. The prairie was named after Seecoffee's son, King Payne. The naturalist William Bartram visited Seecoffee in the 1770s. Bartram called him the Cowkeeper, after the huge herds of cattle he kept on the prairie. Seecoffee was an ally to the English and hated the Spanish. When England ceded Florida to Spain in 1783, Seecoffee put an army in the field and advanced on St. Augustine, but died of old age on the way. He was 70.

Cubo Line

In 1705, the Spanish people in St. Augustine started erecting a series of defensive walls to enclose the town. The first part of this system was the Cubo Line, essentially consisting of an earthen and log revetment. The line ran west from the Castillo de San Marcos to the San Sebastian River along the northern edge of the town. The Cubo Line was strengthened and rebuilt repeatedly by both the Spaniards and the British. The City Gate, part of the line, was built in 1808, only a few years before the United States took control of Florida. A portion of the Cubo Line earthen wall was reconstructed in the 1970s.

Fort DePupa

In the early 1700s, the Spanish had an east-west road across north Florida. At the point where the road crossed the St. Johns River, just west of St. Augustine, the Spanish constructed two forts to guard the crossing. On the east bank they constructed Fort Picolata. On the west bank Fort DePupa was built.

Around 1716, an earth platform surrounded by a shallow moat was built, and on the platform a log fort was erected. In 1739 the fort was enlarged. The fort was large enough to hold a garrison of about fifty men. The fort was attacked several times by Indians, but the principal engagement, which brought it to fame, was when General James Edward Oglethorpe, governor of the Georgia colony, attacked it just prior to his siege of St. Augustine in 1740. It was the fight at Fort DePupa that alerted the city of St. Augustine and let the Spaniards prepare for the siege.

Since the garrison at Fort DePupa was not a large one, Oglethorpe's forces had very little trouble bringing about its surrender, but the troops in Fort Picolata, across the St. Johns River, heard the attack and sent a runner to St. Augustine. Oglethorpe crossed the river, took Fort Picolata, and then marched away to the stronghold at the Castillo de San Marcos.

The Spanish rebuilt both Fort DePupa and Fort Picolata with two-story coquina buildings with two swivel guns mounted on the roof. British soldiers occupied Fort DePupa during the years Great Britain occupied Florida.

Cubo Defense Line. The Spanish built a log wall known as the Cubo Defense Line to protect St. Augustine. Constructed of palm tree logs and mud, the wall represented the northern boundary of the city. The Castillo de San Marcos is shown in the background.

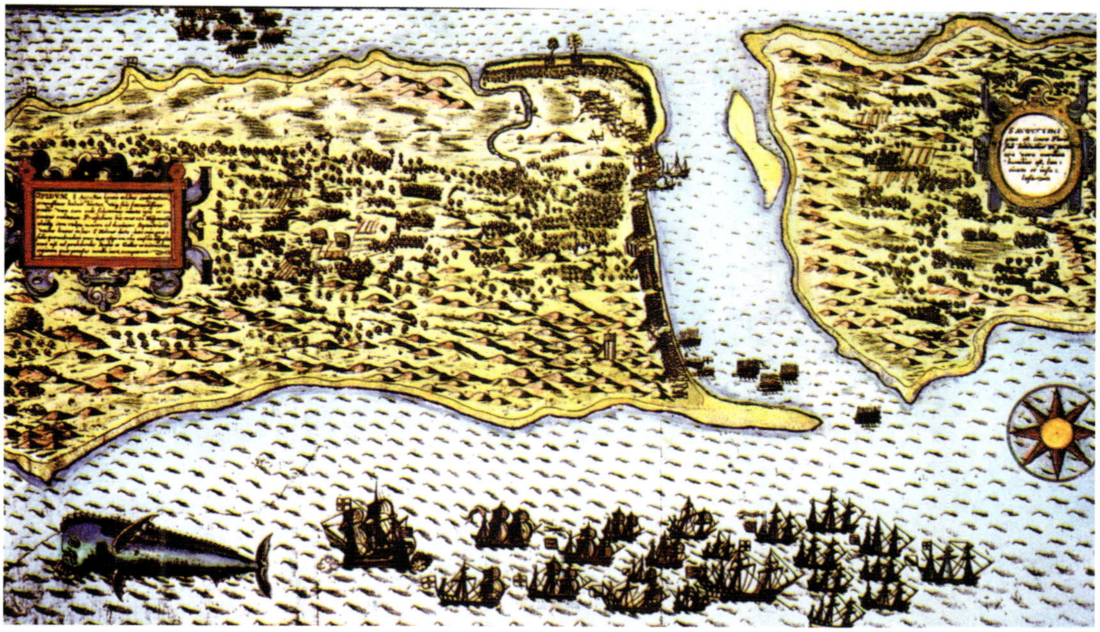

Drake's Attack. Admiral Sir Francis Drake, famous sea rover and privateer, was encouraged by England's Queen Elizabeth to attack Spanish ships as they sailed between Spain and the New World. This drawing shows Drake's fleet and 2,000 men attacking the Spanish settlement of St. Augustine in June 1586. Drake destroyed the wood fort San Juan de Pinos, and burned and pillaged the town.

Drake's Attack of St. Augustine

In 1586, the English admiral and explorer Sir Francis Drake arrived off St. Augustine. He immediately landed his troops on Anastasia Island, intending to make an attack the next day. During the night, however, the Spaniards fled from the fort, leaving behind fourteen pieces of brass ordinance and 2,000 pounds sterling, which had been sent to pay the soldiers. Upon learning that the soldiers had fled, Drake immediately crossed the bay, and then plundered and destroyed the fort. To attack the town, owing to marsh and streams south of the fort they found it necessary to take to the boats and row south. On landing, a Spaniard fired from ambush, killing Drake's sergeant-major. In retaliation for this Drake burned the town and destroyed the gardens. After the departure of Drake, the Spaniards rebuilt the fort. This fort was built of wood and earth, part of an octagon in shape

Fort Gadsden

A fort was built in late 1814 by Lieutenant Colonel Edward Nichols, of the British Marines, as a rallying point to encourage the Seminole Indians to ally themselves with England against the United States. The fort was first called a British Post and later Fort Nichols. It was used as a headquarters for negotiations with Indians and Blacks.

In 1815, when the British withdrew from the area, the fort, including its artillery and military supplies, was given to the Seminoles and Blacks who had moved into it, seeking the protection it offered and cultivating successful and profitable plantations around it. The fortification became known as Negro Fort and it served as a beacon light to restless and rebellious slaves.

Its location in Spanish Florida did not deter Major General Andrew Jackson from ordering its elimination as a threat to American commerce on the Apalachicola River. On July 27, 1816, Lieutenant Colonel Duncan L. Clinch, with U.S. forces and 150 Creek Indians, fired on the fort and destroyed it with a "hot shot" cannon ball that exploded in the powder magazine (ammunition area) killing all but fifty of the 320 occupants. Later, upon inspection, the fort was found to contain ten cannons, 2,500 stands of musket, 500 carbines, and 500 swords.

In 1818, with the first violent episode at the fort still fresh in everyone's mind, Andrew Jackson led a force down the Apalachicola River to destroy Seminole villages in what is called the First Seminole War (1817-1818). Impressed by the strategic location of the old fort, Jackson instructed Lieutenant James Gadsden to build a new fortification there as a supply base. Inspired by the Lieutenant's zeal, Jackson named the fort in Gadsden's honor.

Fort George

Originally built by English forces under the command of General John Campbell in 1779, Fort George was continuously garrisoned to defend Pensacola, the English capital of West Florida. The Spanish, under Don Bernardo De Galvez, bombarded the fort on April 27, 1781. On May 8th, a Spanish shell struck the power magazine and fifty men were killed and many more wounded in the explosion. General Campbell had little choice but to surrender. He dictated his surrender terms to Galvez. The number of British prisoners taken was 1,113. The number of Spanish soldiers lost was seventy-four men killed and 198 wounded.

In 1783, the Spanish dismantled and reconstructed Fort George, renaming it Fort San Miguel. Constructed of earth and timber, the fort soon fell into complete disrepair after the bombardment by General Andrew Jackson in 1814.

Dominique de Gourgues' Revenge

In 1565, Pedro Menendez had 245 French Huguenot prisoners put to death on the beaches at Mazantas, fourteen miles south of St. Augustine. There was a gentleman in France, Dominique de Gourgues, who could not rest until the massacre of his countrymen was revenged. He secretly fitted out three small vessels, sailed with nearly two hundred men in August 1567, and after a very stormy voyage reached Cuba. The Spaniards were more strongly situated in Florida than the French had been. St. Augustine was well defended, a new fort, called San Mateo, had been built on the site of Fort Caroline, and there were two small forts guarding the mouth of the St. Johns River. De Gourgues sailed from Cuba, joined forces with Saturiwa, a powerful Timucua Indian Chief, and destroyed the Spanish forts. St. Augustine was too strong to be attacked, so when the forts were destroyed, farewells were said to the Timucua Indian allies, and the ships of revenge sailed for home. Upon their return to France, the Huguenots greeted De Gourgues warmly; however, the king and nobles were not pleased. The king of Spain demanded his life and he was obliged to live in concealment for several years. Things later grew brighter for him. He died years later, just as he was about to take command of a Portuguese fleet against his old enemies, the Spaniards.

Green Cross of Florida

In 1817, the Scottish adventurer General Gregor MacGregor led a ragtag army of seventy-eight men that hoped to capture Amelia Island and create such a turmoil that the United States would take over the colony in order to restore order. The plan was similar to that of the Patriots in 1812. MacGregor's army captured the island and raised their flag, the "Green Cross of Florida."

However, due to lack of money and adequate reinforcements, he left his lieutenants in charge. The lieutenants made a deal with a French privateer, Luis Aury, in order to maintain control. Airy, in exchange for his support, demanded command of the island and, on September 21, 1817, raised the flag of the revolutionary Republic of Mexico, under whose sanction he was currently acting. The island then entered a period of bedlam. The United States sent gunboats and Marines to take control in trust for Spain.

Fort Guana

A Spanish defense, Fort Guana was built in the late 1700s several miles north of St. Augustine.

Horseshoe Bend Battle

On May 27, 1814, General Andrew Jackson met a major force of Creek Indians at Tohopeka (Horseshoe Bend) on the Tallapoosa River in Alabama. His victory in this battle completely broke the power of the Creeks as a nation. Many of them went to Pensacola to the British; others moved into the interior of Florida.

Fort Marion

In 1821, Florida and the Castillo de San Marcos in St. Augustine came into American hands through a treaty. On July 10th the Spanish flag came down and the twenty-three starred flag of the United States rose over the old embattlements. In 1824 Congress ordered the name of the Castillo changed to Fort Marion. This was to honor General Francis Marion of South Carolina, known as the famous "Swamp Fox" of the Revolutionary War.

Through much of the 1800s, Fort Marion was a military prison. The last real military use was as a prison during the Spanish-American War. In 1942, Congress restored the fort's original Spanish name.

Fort Matanzas

Since its founding in 1565, the military outpost town of St. Augustine had been the heart of Spain's coastal defenses in Florida. In 1569, Pedro Menendez built a wooden watchtower and a thatched hut at Matanzas Inlet to house six soldiers who would take turns scanning the horizon. If a ship was sighted, a runner or a man in a log canoe set out to warn St. Augustine. Watching and warning was the tower's only task, for it lacked any armament. After the completion of the Castillo de San Marcos in 1695, the town had only one weakness: fourteen miles to the south, Matanzas Inlet allowed access to the Matanzas River, by which enemy vessels could attack the town from the rear — out of range of the Castillo's cannons. In 1740-1742, the Spanish built Fort Matanzas on Rattlesnake Island near the Matanzas Inlet.

Fort Matanzas. Located on Rattlesnake Island, this water-surrounded stone fort, with the bloody name of Matanzas (Spanish for "massacre"), guarded the southern entrance to St. Augustine. A sturdy masonry structure with a minaret-like sentry box, it has been a National Monument since 1924 and is accessible only by boat.

A Decaying Fort Matanzas. Fort Matanzas was built by the Spanish in 1740-1742. Neglected for many years, this postcard shows how the fort looked at the beginning of the 20th century.

Fort McIntosh

Built by the British during the American Revolution, Fort McIntosh was located on the south bank of the St. Marys River, on the old Oakland Plantation. The Battle of Cabbage Swamp was fought near the fort in 1778.

Menendez Fort

Upon arrival in Florida in 1565, Spanish leader Pedro Menendez and his soldiers destroyed the French settlement at Fort Caroline, near Jacksonville. Menendez then moved his soldiers and settlers to the St. Augustine area where the Seloy tribe of Timucua Indians had a settlement. Chief Seloy gave over the great house, a huge circular thatched structure capable of holding several hundred people, to the Spaniards. It was around this huge meetinghouse that Menendez built a fort. A moat, fourteen feet wide and three feet deep, was dug around the house. Additional fortifications of a breastwork and wooden palisade were added, to protect the munitions and stores. Several hundred more members of the Spanish force established a camp or village just north of the fort.

Relations between the Spanish and Seloy tribe deteriorated and after seven months the Timucua Indians burned the great house and fort. In 1570 the Spanish settlement moved to the Castillo de San Marcos site near downtown St. Augustine.

The original Menendez Fort site (the Seloy meetinghouse) is thought to be located in part of the present day grounds of the Fountain of Youth Park and the Roman Catholic shrine of Nuestra Senora de la Leche.

Menendez Fort. This drawing is of Timucua Indian Chief Seloy's great house after fortification by Spanish conquistador Pedro Menendez and his troops.

Moore's Attack of St. Augustine

In 1702, Governor James Moore, of South Carolina, sent an expedition consisting of 600 militia and the same number of Indians against St. Augustine. Part of the expedition under Colonel Davis came by land, attacked and took immediate possession of the town, with the troops and inhabitants retiring to the Castillo de San Marcos. Governor Moore arrived shortly after with a naval force, but owing to the lack of heavy siege guns, no impression on the fort could be made. After a siege of fifty days, Moore returned to South Carolina. Before he retired, he committed the barbarity of burning the town, as noted in the above image.

Fort Mose

Located two miles north of St. Augustine, the fortress had log walls reinforced with an earthen berm. It enclosed thatched huts and was ringed with a ditch containing "prickly palmetto royal."

Fort Moultrie

During the English occupation of Florida (1763-1783) Lieutenant Governor John Moultrie built a plantation on the Matanzas River, south of St. Augustine. In 1815, during the Second Spanish occupation of Florida, the area became a Spanish land grant to Bautista Don Ferreira. The site was awarded in 1817 to Martin Hernandez for military services. Martin's son, Joseph Martin Hernandez, who also owned several other plantations in the area, developed it as the Bella Vista Plantation. Bella Vista was fortified in the 1820s and later a regular fort was constructed here and operated as an outpost for St. Augustine. Here, on September 18, 1823, was executed the Treaty of Moultrie Creek between the U.S. Government and the Seminole Indians.

Narvaez Comes to Florida

On April 15, 1528, Spanish explorer Panfilo Narvaez landed with 400 men and some horses in the vicinity of present day Tampa. After settling on the shore, he sent one of his ships to Cuba for more supplies. The remaining three ships sailed north up the coast of the Gulf of Mexico while Narvaez took a group by land in the same direction.

Indian Hostility

Narvaez and the colonists encountered hostile Timucua Indians, but they also found some gold specimens that greatly excited the Spaniards. The Timucua Indians told them that the gold came from the land of Apalachee, the Tallahassee area today. The Spaniards quickly departed overland for Apalachee.

As Narvaez and his band pushed northward, they met with increasing hostility from the Timucua Indians. There were few trails suitable to horses and armed men, and it often took several days just to find a passage through Florida's deep swamps or hammocks (dense jungle-like areas). Thunderstorms and windstorms hampered progress, and insects plagued the group day and night. They found no gold, and when they finally reached the coast at

Narvaez Lands in the Tampa Bay Area.

Indians Kill Narvaez. In 1528, Spanish leader and conquistador Panfilo Narvaez and his soldiers met hostile Timucua Indians as they marched through Florida. These explorers were probably the first Europeans in the area. The Narvaez expedition suffered many hardships; Narvaez was killed, and most of his soldiers died.

Apalachee, they found no ships and no supplies waiting for them. The group sailing along the coast had mistaken the meeting place and returned to Cuba after searching unsuccessfully for their companions on the land.

Fate of the Expedition

It was many years before anyone learned the fate of Narvaez's expedition. Indians had killed Narvaez. His treasurer, Cabeza de Vaca, with about 240 men, began a journey to join the Spanish in Mexico. Eight years later, De Vaca, a black man named Esteban, and two others walked into Mexico City — they were the sole survivors of the Narvaez expedition. De Vaca later wrote a full account of the expedition in Florida.

Fort Negro

The events that occurred in Florida from 1815 to 1818 did not augur well for Spain. During these years Florida was invaded by many forces. The first of these attacks came from the United States in 1816. During the war the British had built and equipped a fort on the Apalachicola River. The British fort at Prospect Bluff, fifteen miles up the river from the Gulf of Mexico, had earthworks, two bastions, a powder magazine, and sported twelve cannons. They left guns, ammunition, and other equipment there when they retired from Florida. The fort was soon in the possession of blacks, mostly runaway slaves who were friends of the Seminole Indians. It was known as Fort Negro (or Negro Fort) and became a center for launching raids against Spanish and American settlers; it also served as a magnet for other runaway slaves.

The United States demanded Spain suppress this activity, but Spain was too weak to comply. After a supply convoy heading for Fort Scott (a U.S. fort on the Florida-Georgia border) was fired upon, the United States attacked and blew up the fort July 27, 1816, killing all but fifty of the 320 blacks and Seminoles inside the fort. A shot fired from a U.S. gunboat fell directly into the fort's magazine of almost 700 kegs of powder. It was a large explosion.

Fort Newnan

A United States Army post during the Patriot's War, Fort Newnan was established in 1812 near the St. Johns River in northeast Florida. Colonel Daniel Newnan used the fort during an engagement with the Alachua Seminole Indians under their leader King Payne, who was killed during the battle.

Ocali Indians Battle the Spanish

In 1528, Spanish conquistador and explorer Panfilo Narvaez led a force of 400 armored men, some mounted on horses also clad in armor, into the wilds of Florida. News of this invasion reached Ocali (present-day Ocala) and a force of several hundred warriors was sent to oppose the Spanish invaders. The Ocali warriors, a subgroup of Timucua Indians, met Narvaez's expedition and a short but fierce battle resulted. The Indians were defeated, their primitive weapons useless against Spanish armor and bullets. Savage dogs deployed against the Indians by the Spanish horsemen terrified the natives. The Spaniards, looking for gold, left Ocali and marched north toward the province of Apalache.

Eleven years later, on May 30, 1539, more than 600 infantry and cavalry led by Spanish conquistador Hernando DeSoto landed near Tampa Bay and immediately headed for the large Indian town of Ocali. After many adventures with the Indians, DeSoto raided the village's food warehouses and pushed ahead toward Apalache.

Oglethorpe Battery Park

A half block grass lot located in St. Augustine, the center of Oglethorpe Battery Park features a stone monument commemorating the historic event that occurred here. From this site, British troops led by General James Oglethorpe, Governor of the colony of Georgia, bombarded the Castillo de San Marcos for nearly a month (June 27 to July 20, 1740). The Castillo's massive coquina walls absorbed the cannon shot, and the fortress consequently suffered only minor damage. The battle eventually resulted in Oglethorpe and his troops withdrawing to Georgia.

Palmer's Attack

In 1727, Colonel Palmer of Carolina, crossed the Attamaha River with 300 white troopers and a large band of Indians. He laid waste all northern Florida, to the gates of St. Augustine.

Patriots of East Florida

Under orders from President James Madison, George Mathews, former governor of Georgia, planned an invasion of Spanish East Florida. He selected John Houstoun McIntosh to lead the rebellion. The plan was simple. The "Patriots of East Florida," as they styled themselves, would quickly capture East Florida and immediately offer it to the United States. The U.S. would accept the offer, in part, because Spain owed the country five million dollars in spoliation claims.

The Patriots met March 13, 1812, proclaimed their independence, and extended an invitation for all men

Pensacola in the British Period. In 1763, Pensacola consisted of around 100 huts and minor fortifications. The town served as capital of British West Florida for nearly two decades.

in East Florida who wanted freedom to join them. The Patriot flag displayed a soldier in blue with a white background.

Four days later, some 180 Patriots landed on Amelia Island. The Spanish troops, a small force of nine men, surrendered to the Patriot "army." Shortly afterwards the Patriots offered to Mathews, all of East Florida between the St. Johns and St. Marys rivers, including the coastal islands. Mathews accepted the offer and U.S. troops shortly occupied Fernandina. The Patriot "army" then headed for St. Augustine, but Spanish governor Juan de Estrada stubbornly refused to surrender the city. Subsequently President Madison disavowed the actions by Mathews and the Patriots, but U.S. troops were not withdrawn. The Patriots were eventually driven from East Florida.

The Patriots were not successful in their efforts to establish an East Florida government, but they helped instill in many Americans the idea that the Floridas must eventually belong to the United States.

Pensacola

As the largest safe harbor between Tampa Bay and Mobile, Pensacola Bay was well known to Spanish pilots early in the sixteenth century. Tristan DeLuna's attempt to establish Florida's first permanent colony in 1559 failed when a hurricane destroyed more than half of the fleet's eleven vessels. Strategically, a settlement at Pensacola would help protect Spanish outposts in Mexico, but no permanent occupation was possible until 1698. When Great Britain obtained control of Florida in 1763, the town consisted of around one hundred huts and several minor fortifications. As in East Florida, the British were more successful at establishing a viable town; Pensacola served as capital of British West Florida for nearly two decades.

In 1814, the British used the harbor as a base in their war with the United States, but withdrew when the city was attacked by General Andrew Jackson. Under lax Spanish control, Pensacola became a base for Indian attacks on the Georgia settlements. In 1818 Jackson again invaded Florida, captured the city and held it until the following year when Spain sent troops to check the Indian disorders.

It was in Pensacola, in 1821, that Andrew Jackson completed the transaction in which Spain sold Florida to the United States. This was the capital until 1822 and Jackson lived here as first territorial governor. A Navy Yard was established in 1825. Fort Barrancas was built between 1839 and 1844 in back of Fort San Carlos. By 1860, Pensacola was the largest city in the state.

The Capture of Pensacola. Bernardo de Galvez, governor of Spanish Louisiana, led the naval attack on Gulf ports and the successful Spanish siege of Pensacola in 1781. The engraving by M. Ponce and M. Godefrey gives an imaginative view of this battle.

Pensacola Battle

As the American Revolution progressed, the British developed a strategy to trap the American patriots by attacking the thirteen original Colonies from all sides. Anticipating an English assault on Spanish Louisiana, its governor, Colonel Bernardo de Galvez, began planning a counteroffensive in 1777. He hoped to strike the British before they had an opportunity to attack Louisiana. Colonel Galvez made plans to recapture West Florida, once a part of the old Spanish colony of Florida. His aim was to control the most important British port cities along the Gulf of Mexico and on the Mississippi River. This would prevent the English from using the ports to supply their own troops.

In June 1779, Spain declared war on England. For the next two years Galvez conducted a series of successful military operations against British outposts along the Mississippi River and the Gulf of Mexico. Galvez had control of the waterways, thus eliminating the British from using the waterways to attack Americans without fear of an enemy attack.

On March 9, 1781, with thirty-two vessels and 1,315 men, Galvez landed on Santa Rosa Island, across the harbor from Pensacola, and began a two-month siege. Reinforcements arrived March 22, giving Galvez 3,857 troops under his command. Soon after he began his attack on Pensacola.

Realizing Galvez's intention, Brigadier General John Campbell evacuated the town. On April 19, Spanish soldiers numbering 1,600 arrived from Havana on eighteen ships. With them came French vessels carrying 725 troops. Four days later another 3,675 Spanish soldiers came ashore, increasing Galvez's forces to 9,857 men.

On Santa Rosa Island, Galvez's troops built a small earthen fort called San Bernardo. On May 6, Galvez began a land and sea bombardment of Pensacola. Two days into the battle, a shot from one of the Spanish cannons hit a powder magazine of one of the British fortifications. Amid the huge explosion, the Spanish captured an English redoubt. This action left another British defense, Fort George, totally exposed to Spanish fire. With only about 1,600 troops, General Campbell surrendered Pensacola to the Spanish.

The Battle of Pensacola, the last major Spanish victory over the British, was one of the most important battles of the American Revolutionary War. None of the men who took part wore the American uniform. Yet, the Spanish capture of Pensacola saved the Gulf of Mexico and the Mississippi River from British domination and gave the American patriots an advantage in the region.

Pensacola Navy Yard

After the War of 1812, the United States decided to build forts at all major harbors. When Florida was added to the country in 1821, Pensacola was selected for a Navy Yard. To protect that yard, four forts would be built: Pickens on Santa Rosa Island; McRee on Perdido Key; Barrancas and Advanced Redoubt (Fort Redoubt) on the mainland. The work went on for thirty years beginning in 1829.

Fort Pickens

Fort Pickens, a massive, five-sided fortification on Santa Rosa Island, was built soon after Spain ceded Florida to the United States in 1821. The fort protected an important naval shipyard on Pensacola Bay. Fort Pickens was one of three forts built to guard the entrance of Pensacola Bay. Fort Pickens covers the western end of Santa Rosa Island. It is the best known of the three fortresses, including Fort McRee on Perdido Key, which has mostly deteriorated over time from the weather, and restored Fort Barrancas across Pensacola Bay at the Naval Air Station.

The seven-acre, Fort Pickens was named for Brigadier General Andrew Pickens who commanded South Carolina soldiers in the Revolutionary War. Its cost was $759,168; at one time it was the second largest fort in the U.S.

Construction of this coastal fortification began in 1829 and was completed in 1834. Gun emplacements for cannons were mounted within and on top of its walls, which were constructed of locally made brick. The moated fort has intact walls forty feet high and twelve feet thick. Twenty million bricks were used to build the structure.

Fort Pickens. Located on Santa Rosa Island near Pensacola, Fort Pickens was begun in 1829, and completed in 1834, when it was garrisoned by an artillery company of thirty-four men. It was designed to mount 250 guns and to accommodate a garrison of 600 men during ordinary warfare or 1,200 men under siege. However, prior to the Civil War the average number of soldiers was about fifty.

Cannons at Fort Pickens. Brought to Pensacola during the period from 1765-1781 by the British, these cannons were used in defense of the town by the British, Spanish, United States, and Confederate States.

1950s View of Fort Pickens.

Fort Picolata

In the early 1700s, the Spanish built Fort Picolata at the present day town of Picolata, on the east bank of the St. Johns River, and Fort DePupa on the west bank of the river. These forts were located at a strategic juncture, where the river narrows. These two forts were outlying defenses of St. Augustine, which was located about twenty miles to the east.

In 1740, General James Oglethorpe, governor of Georgia, and his troops captured both forts on his way to attack the Castillo de San Marcos in St. Augustine. Fort Picolata was burned to the ground during this invasion. The fort was later rebuilt with a 30-foot high tower. In 1765, the British signed a treaty at Fort Picolata with Indians that defined the limits of British-Indian settlements. The fort was abandoned in 1769.

Fort Piribiriba

Built by the Spanish after Governor James Moore of South Carolina invaded Florida in 1702, Fort Piribiriba was located at the mouth of the St. Johns River, near present day Jacksonville.

Ponce de Leon Battles the Calusa Indians

On April 2, 1513, Spanish explorer and soldier Juan Ponce de Leon landed his ships on the Atlantic coast and claimed the land for the King of Spain. After spending a short time along the Atlantic coast, Ponce de Leon's three ships sailed south through the Florida Keys (Florida Strait) and into the Gulf of Mexico. Sometime around May 23, 1513, the party attempted to land near Charlotte Harbor on the west coast, but they were driven off by hostile Calusa Indians. Ponce de Leon returned to Puerto Rico. It was eight years before he made any further attempts to take command of his territory named Florida.

In 1521, Ponce de Leon returned to Florida. This time, he sailed along the lower southwestern coast and landed in the Port Charlotte area. There he tried to establish a settlement for Spain with colonists, cattle, and seeds that he had brought with him. Soon the Calusa Indians had attacked the little settlement. Ponce de Leon was wounded, but escaped with some of the people from the settlement. Though they reached Cuba safely, Ponce de Leon died within a few days of the wounds the Indians had inflicted.

Potano-Outina Indian Battle

The Potano (Potanou) and Outina (Utina) Indians were sub-tribes of the Timucua Indians. These large, powerful tribes were also bitter enemies. When a French colony settled at the mouth of the St. Johns River in 1564, Outina persuaded some of the French soldiers to join him in an attack on Potano. In the battle that followed many of the Potano chiefs and warriors were killed or enslaved and a number of villages devastated.

Fort Quartel

This Spanish fort was established around 1575 on the north bank of the Matanzas River, near St. Augustine.

Quesada Battery

Designed to prevent the passage up St. Johns River by enemy vessels, the Quesada Battery, a Spanish fortification, was established around 1793 at the mouth of the river.

Royal Navy Redoubt

The natural advantages of this location have inspired engineers of three nations to build forts. In 1763, the British built the first fort on a bluff overlooking the entrance to Pensacola Bay. In 1761, a Spanish fleet under General Bernardo de Galvez sailed past the Royal Navy Redoubt, manned by a force of British sailors and German mercenaries, to capture Pensacola. The Spanish built a stronger fort, completed in 1797, called Fort San Carlos. America built Fort Barrancas on this bluff in 1839-1844.

Fort San Antonio de Padua

Early in 1566 the governor of Florida, Pedro Menendez, arrived in San Carlos Bay, near present day Fort Myers, with a large expeditionary force consisting of seven vessels to deal with Carlos, the supreme ruler of the Calusa Indians in southwest Florida. Carlos seemed friendly at first and even offered his sister as a wife to cement the relationship. Eager to please, Menendez promptly married her in a mock ceremony and then made arrangements for a fort and mission to be built on the island (Estero Island) where Carlos had his headquarters. Later that year Menendez sent a body of soldiers and colonists, to build and occupy the fort, naming it Fort St. Antonio de Padua. In the meantime, relations with Carlos had deteriorated and the fort was completed with some difficulty. After less than a year the fort became untenable due to the hostility of the Indians. Menendez later moved his forces to a nearby island (probably Sanibel Island) that afforded better defense against attack from the Calusa Indians. After Menendez's forces abandoned Fort San Antonio, the Calusa Indians wasted no time burning the fort.

Fort San Bernardo

The Queen's Redoubt in Pensacola was built by the British during their occupation of Florida (1763-1783). When the Spanish started occupying Florida for the second time, they renamed the fortification Fort San Bernardo. The fort, a semicircular network of batteries connected by trenches, was located several hundred yards northwest of Fort George. In the early nineteenth century, the fort was in complete disrepair.

Fort San Carlos

(Amelia Island)

Built in 1816 on a bluff overlooking the Amelia River in what is present day Fernandina Beach, the fort, made of wood and earthworks, was armed with eight or ten guns. As the Spanish Empire disintegrated, Fort San Carlos became increasingly vulnerable to foreign intervention. Commissioned by representatives of revolting South American countries to liberate Florida from Spanish control, Scottish soldier of fortune, General Gregor MacGregor seized the fort in June 1817. After his withdrawal in September, the Spanish attempt to reassert their authority was repelled by forces led by MacGregor's lieutenants, Jared Irwin and Ruggles Hubbard. Somewhat later, the pirate Luis Aury gained control of the fort. Because Aury's privateering threatened negotiations concerning the cession of Florida, United States troops occupied Fort San Carlos in December 1817. Although upset by U.S. interference at Fort San Carlos, Spain did cede Florida in 1821, and the U.S. abandoned the fort shortly after the transfer.

Fort San Carlos. An aerial view of the seventeenth century Fort Carlos (circular structure in the foreground) and the more modern Fort Barrancas, which was built by the U.S. Government during the nineteenth century. The two forts are connected by an underground tunnel.

Fort San Carlos Today.

Ruins of Fort San Carlos. Built by the Spanish General Andreas de Arriola in 1781-1790 to guard the entrance to Pensacola Bay and protect the settlement he established around the fort. During the wars of the eighteenth century between England, France and Spain the old fort changed hands many times.

Fort San Carlos

(Pensacola)

Located on the Naval Air Station overlooking West Pensacola Bay, Fort San Carlos is one of the early fortifications in this area and has played an important part in Florida's history. This massive 100 by 100 foot Spanish semicircular brick fort, with a dry moat on the forward semicircular side, was erected between 1781 and 1790.

During the War of 1812 the British captured the fort with the intention of using it against the United States, but General Andrew Jackson took the fort from them in two days of fierce fighting. In 1814 the fort was returned to Spain. Four years later, 1818, when the Seminoles rose up against the United States, General Jackson again took over Fort San Carlos, so it could not be used against him, again returning it to Spain at the end of hostilities in 1819.

Fort San Carlos became the property of the United States when Spain ceded Florida to the United States in 1821. The fort was later modified and became the Water Battery for Fort Barrancas.

Fort San Diego

In 1736, Diego de Espinosa owned a cattle ranch on Diego Plains, a flat, open area about twenty miles northwest of St. Augustine. For protection against Indians, his house was surrounded by a fifteen-foot high palisade with two bastions at opposite corners. Manned later by Spanish soldiers, this post was known as Fort San Diego. On May 23, 1740, during the British expedition against St. Augustine, General James Oglethorpe's 400-man army captured the fort and its fifty defenders. The British added a ditch and breastwork, and used the fort to protect the St. Johns River-St. Augustine supply line. Upon their departure from Florida, the British destroyed the fortifications, but the Spanish quickly returned and rebuilt them. In 1743 approximately two hundred Indians and a number of British militiamen destroyed the fort and killed forty Spanish defenders. The fort was never subsequently rebuilt. By late 1743 the fort lay in ruins.

Fort San Fernando

In 1686, the Spanish built Fort San Fernando in present day Old Town in Fernandina Beach on Amelia Island. In 1702, Governor James Moore, of South Carolina, and a force of English militia and Creek Indians, invaded north Florida, overran Amelia Island, and captured Fort San Fernando. Moore and his forces went on to, unsuccessfully, attack the Castillo de San Marcos in St. Augustine. After a three-month blockade of St. Augustine, Moore returned to South Carolina.

Fort San Juan

Erected in 1565 by Spanish conquistador Pedro Menendez on Little Talbot Island, several miles south of Amelia Island, the fort was designed to help guard the St. Johns River and Fort San Mateo (formerly Fort Caroline). In 1567, Frenchman Dominique de Gourgues, with 180 French followers, seized the island, destroyed Fort San Juan, and went on to destroy Fort San Mateo...in revenge for the Fort Caroline massacre by Menendez.

San Juan De Pinos

During the century before the coquina rock Castillo de San Marcos fort was started, nine wooden forts, one after another, were built at St. Augustine. One of these wooden forts, San Juan de Pinos, was burned by the English freebooter Francis Drake in 1586, after being robbed of its bronze artillery and some 2,000 pounds sterling in the most devastating raid St. Augustine ever suffered. The fort consisted of a pine timber stockade around small buildings for gunpowder storage and quarters. Cannons were mounted atop a broad platform, called a caballero, so that they could fire over the stockade. Wood forts like San Juan de Pinos were only temporary as the humid climate, Indian fire arrows, and seasonal hurricanes limited their useful life.

Fort San Lucia

Spanish conquistador Pedro Menendez built this fort in 1568 in the vicinity of present day Jensen Beach. Although Menendez left a garrison at the fort, Indians killed so many of his soldiers the survivors retreated to St. Augustine.

Fort San Luis De Apalachee

The Apalachee Indian chiefdom was one of the most powerful and wealthy in Florida. They had well-established systems of government and religion led by chiefs and priests who presided over community activities and maintained contact with other chiefdoms over a greater distance. As early as 1607, Apalachee chiefs asked the Spanish governor of Florida to send friars to their province.

Established by the Spanish military authorities and Franciscan friars in 1640, Fort San Luis De Apalachee and a mission known as San Luis De Talimali was located on one of the region's highest hilltops just west of present day downtown Tallahassee. San Luis was one of more than 100 mission settlements established in Spanish Florida between the 1560s and 1690s. The mission was second in importance

Fort San Luis De Apalachee. In the 1690s, the Spaniards and Apalachee Indians built a fort on one of the highest hilltops just west of present-day downtown Tallahassee.

Fort St. Luis. A team of oxen and handlers approach the entrance to the fort with a cannon and ammunition.

only to St. Augustine. San Luis was recognized as the military, religious, and administrative capital of western Florida.

Fort San Luis De Apalachee served as the headquarters for seven missionary settlements in the present day Tallahassee area, the western region of Spanish Florida. During the half century that San Luis evolved and developed, a series of blockhouses were built, before the "genuine fort" was erected in the 1690s when the threat of British attack became imminent. The fort had four features:

- The blockhouse
- A surrounding palisade with bastions
- A dry moat
- A covered way

The military engineer-builder (and Deputy Governor) was Captain Jacinto Roque Perez.

The number of Spanish soldiers stationed at San Luis ranged from twelve to forty-five. There were also an unknown number of civilians who remained on call in the event of a military strike.

The Apalachee Indians provided the bulk of the province's military power and received training in the use of firearms from the Spaniards. They served as sentries and some held military titles, outnumbering Spanish soldiers on raids.

Archaeology investigations have turned up the following details about the fort: the two-story blockhouse had massive wattle-and-daub walls, whitewashed with lime and strong enough to support the cannon on its roof. The blockhouse was 40 by 70 feet, partitioned into a guardroom, troop quarters, and warehouses. The

The Fort. The Spanish garrison stationed at Fort San Luis was always small, ranging from twelve to forty-five men; however, its numbers could be supplemented by Spanish civilians and Apalachee Indian warriors.

palisade, with four diamond-shaped bastions, measured 130 by 230 feet, and was eleven feet high. The dry moat was three to five feet deep, planted with prickly pear cactus or other thorny plants as an added deterrent. The covered way led down into the ravine, where there was a water source.

Beginning in 1702, British Carolina Governor James Moore began a full-scale attack on Spanish Florida aimed at St. Augustine and the missions along the Atlantic coast. Then, in early 1704, Moore mounted a campaign against missions in the Apalachee Indian area. With fifty volunteers and 1,000 Creek Indians, he raided the missions, severely damaging them. Many of the Apalachee Indians were taken captive as slaves.

The strongly fortified San Luis was not a target of the initial raids of 1704. On July 31st, two days before the final strike force reached San Luis, the Spanish and Apalachee Indians evacuated and burned the mission in order to prevent British forces from occupying it. Women and children were the first to be evacuated while the men stayed behind to burn it. The fort was the last structure to be destroyed before San Luis was abandoned.

Mission Destroyed.
In 1704, the Spaniards and Apalachee Indians evacuated and burned Mission San Luis. The mission and fort were burned in order to prevent approaching British forces from occupying them.

Apalachee Indian Warriors. They raided a Chisca Indian Village in 1677.

Building the Fort. After completion of a new, two-story blockhouse in the 1690s, an eleven-foot high palisade with four diamond shaped bastions was built.

San Marcos De Apalache

During the past four centuries numerous New World travelers have staked their claim at historic San Marcos de Apalache (Fort St. Marks). The site's history began in 1528 when Spanish explorer Panfilo Narvaez arrived with 300 men. Having traveled overland from Tampa, Narvaez, impressed by the area located at the confluence of the Wakulla and St. Marks rivers, built and launched the first ships made by white men in the New World.

In 1539, Hernando De Soto, along with 600 men, followed the same route taken by Narvaez. Banners were hung in the trees near the river to easily mark the river's entrance. (A lighthouse now stands near the site.)

By 1679, the Spanish Governor of Florida started construction on the first fort built at the junction of two rivers. Fort San Marcos was located strategically at the confluence of the Wakulla and St. Marks Rivers. The logs used were coated with lime to give the appearance of stone. The fort had stood only three years when it was burned and looted by French pirates. Not until 1718 did Captain Jose Primo de Ribera arrive to construct a second wooden fort.

Construction was begun on the first stone fort in 1739. Progress was slow, and the fort was less than half complete when it was delivered to the English in 1763 as a result of the war with Spain.

By 1787, Spain regained control of the fort, occupying it for thirteen more years. In 1800, a former British officer named William Augustus Bowles challenged Spanish rule. Bowles attempted to unify and lead an independent Creek nation of four hundred Indians against the Spanish, eventually capturing San Marcos. His rule ended five weeks later when the Spanish returned with a flotilla of nine ships to retake the fort.

Because of continuous Indian raids in Georgia from Spanish Florida, General Andrew Jackson invaded the territory in 1818 and took San Marcos. Two captured British citizens, Robert Arbrister and Alexander Arbuthnot, were tried and found guilty of inciting Indian raids. Jackson executed both men, creating a diplomatic crisis between the United States and Great Britain. Jackson withdrew from San Marcos, leaving the fort once again in Spanish hands.

In 1821, Florida was ceded to the United States, and U.S. troops were sent to occupy the fort. Three years later, the fort was abandoned and turned over to the Territory of Florida. By 1839, the fort was returned to the U.S. Government and construction of a federal marine hospital began eighteen years later, utilizing stones from the Spanish fort. The hospital, which was finished in a year, provided much needed care for victims of yellow fever.

San Marcos De Apalache. In 1679 this Spanish fort was built at the junction of the St. Marks and Wakulla rivers. The logs used were coated with whitewash to give the appearance of stone.

Fort San Miguel

Established by the Spanish in 1757 on the site of the present Historic District in Pensacola, the official name of the fort was Presidio San Miguel de Panzacola, but was commonly referred to as Panzacola, after the Indians who lived in the area.

A stockade on three sides enclosed a space 365 by 700 feet. The fourth side, on the banks of Pensacola Bay, was not palisaded, but had a pier sixty yards long and six yards wide. Located within the stockade were officers' quarters, soldiers' barracks, chapel, gunpowder warehouses, commandant-governor's house, guardhouse, grocery warehouse, and jail.

In 1760, in fear of Indian attack, the Spanish cleared a firing field by destroying the buildings outside the stockade. In August of this year, a hurricane destroyed part of the stockade. Indian attacks continued until Spain ceded Florida to Great Britain in 1763.

The British rebuilt the stockade, anglicized its name to Fort St. Michael, and constructed Fort George north of town. In 1783, after Spain occupied Florida for the second time, they dismantled and reconstructed Fort George, renaming it Fort San Miguel. The fort fell into complete disrepair after the bombardment by General Andrew Jackson in 1814.

Fort San Nicholas

A blockhouse built in 1740 under Spanish governor Don Manuel de Monteano, Fort San Nicholas was located on the south bank of the St. Johns River in present day South Jacksonville. In 1796 John Houston McIntosh, former Revolutionary War officer, led a band of adventurers from Georgia in an attack against Fort San Nicholas, destroying it in revenge for Spanish mistreatment and appropriation of his lands in the area. The fort was later rebuilt, and in 1812, during the Patriots uprising, aroused Americans captured and destroyed the fort. Fort San Nicholas was rebuilt again, and, after the cession of Florida to the United States in 1821, it was maintained principally to prevent smuggling. The fort is enclosed by an excavation 100 feet square. The only memorial to the fort's existence is a gray stone marker about three miles east of U.S. Highway 1 in Jacksonville.

Fort Santa Lucia De Canaveral

This Spanish fort was established in 1568 by Spanish Conquistador Pedro Menendez in the present-day area of Jensen Beach. Soon after the fort's completion, it was besieged by the Ais Indians. With many of the garrison's soldiers killed, the Spanish abandoned the fort.

Fort Santa Maria

A Spanish fort established in the north central part of Amelia Island.

Fort Santa Maria De Galve

This Spanish fort was established prior to 1763 on the Pensacola Bay.

Fort Scott

Built by Brevet Major General Edmund Pendleton Gaines in 1816 at the junction of the Apalachicola, the Chattahoochee, and the Flint rivers, Fort Scott was used to store supplies brought in from New Orleans and to provide defense against Indians. The fort was named in the memory of Lieutenant Richard W. Scott, who was killed by Indians.

Fort Sombrero

The Prince of Wales Redoubt was built by the British during their occupation of Florida. After the successful siege of Pensacola by the Spanish in 1781, the British fortification was renamed Fort Sombrero. The Spanish did not maintain the fort and it soon fell into disrepair.

Spanish Forts

Spanish colonists who settled Florida in the sixteenth to eighteenth centuries had to quickly face the reality of defending their new homes. Their New World not only belonged to Indians, but also was coveted by England, France, and pirates.

They threw up palisades, redoubts, watchtowers, and forts with bastions to protect early settlements, their harbors, and river crossings; to protect these defenses, they fashioned earthworks, palm log revetments, moats, and, for extra good measure, rows of prickly cactus. The wood defense structures perpetually rotted. Coastline erosion and hurricanes destroyed other structures. The colonial forts, moats, palm revetments, wood redoubts, and lookouts are not even a memory anymore; only obscure names in documents or on old maps.

Several colonial masonry forts are still intact, including the Castillo de San Marcos (1695) and Fort Matanzas

(1742), both defending St. Augustine. Forts San Carlos (1797), Fort Pickens (1834), and Fort Barrancas (1844) exist today in Penscola.

Fort St. Andrews

This English outpost was built in 1734-1735 on Cumberland Island during James Edward Oglethorpe's encroachments on Spanish territory.

Fort Stallings

A temporary Patriots War blockhouse, Fort Stallings was established in 1812 on Davis Creek.

St. Augustine

The oldest European settlement in the United States, St. Augustine lies on the Atlantic coast, about forty miles south of the mouth of the St. Johns River. Beginning with the establishment of a small Spanish outpost in 1565, St. Augustine was the focus, and almost, the entire extent, of European occupation in the Florida peninsula for 200 years. Its turbulent and colorful history can be divided into the following periods:

- First Spanish Period (1513-1763)
- British Period (1763-1783)
- Second Spanish Period (1783-1821)
- American Period (1821-present)

St. Augustine City Gates

St. Augustine is bounded by water on the east, west, and south. In the old days its defenders felt there was little danger of attack, except from the north. On this unprotected front were thrown up three defense lines; one west from Fort Mose, about two miles north of the city; one across the peninsula, and the last from Castillo de San Marcos west to the San Sebastian River. The City Gates stood to protect the one entrance to the city. Earthen breastworks, planted on top with impenetrable Spanish bayonet plants, ran from the city wall south along a line as far as the St. Francis Barracks before they swung east to Matanzas Bay.

The City Gate was completed in 1808 as the main entrance to St. Augustine. On either side of the gate was a nine-foot-high earthwork, the Cubo Line, which stretched from the fort west to the San Sebastian River. A portion of the Cubo Line has been reconstructed. Originally, the gate's twin towers of coquina were plastered white with red trim.

Town and Fort. This 1671 view of St. Augustine shows the growing town in the background on the left and the wooden fort on the right. Ships and boats of all kinds filled the port with activity.

City Gate, circa 1880. During the days of Spanish occupation, St. Augustine's inner line of defense consisted of a wall extending from the Castillo de San Marcos to the San Sebastian River. As the town was surrounded on three sides by water, the gate offered, at that time, the only entrance to the city. The City Gate once had heavy doors to seal off the town at night.

Nation's Oldest City. This diorama shows Father Lopez, Spanish diocesan missionary priest, offering the first parish Mass in the United States, September 8, 1565. Pedro Menendez, leader of the Spanish fleet, and his crew surround the altar as they found St. Augustine, our nation's oldest city.

St. Francis Barracks

In 1764, British Governor Grant converted a sixteenth century monastery and church into a barracks for British troops. In 1771, the building was enlarged and named the St. Francis Barracks. After Florida became a territory of the United States, the barracks were occupied by U.S. troops until 1900. Later it was used as the headquarters of Florida's National Guard; the building (shown above) is now the headquarters of the Florida Military Department.

Fort St. Francis de Pupa

A site on the St. Johns River near Green Cove Springs was used as a ferry landing late in the seventeenth century. About 1716, the Spanish built Fort St. Francis de Pupa on this site. It was rebuilt and enlarged early in 1739. The following year English and Indian forces, led by James Oglethorpe, founder of the Georgia colony, captured it. On their withdrawal later in the summer, they destroyed the fort.

Fort St. George

In 1736, General James Edward Oglethorpe, Governor of the colony of Georgia, attacked and occupied San Juan Island and renamed it Fort George Island. There he built a fortification named Fort St. George, basically an earthwork enclosed within a palisade.

Fort Tequesta

In 1567, Spanish explorer Pedro Menendez, the founder of St. Augustine, sent Captain Francisco de Reinoso and Father Juan Rogel to establish a fort and a mission at the main village of the Tequesta Indians in the Miami River/Biscayne Bay area near the present day city of Miami. By 1570 rebellious Tequesta Indians had destroyed the fort.

Thomas Creek Battle

When the American War of Independence began, the new British colonies of East and West Florida did not seek separation from England. East Florida remained comparatively free from serious fighting throughout the course of the Revolutionary War. In the summer of 1777, however, Americans initiated an invasion aimed at capturing St. Augustine. The expedition was composed of Continental Army troops and Georgia militia forces under the command of Lt. Col. Samuel Elbert. Preparations for the defense of east Florida involved the East Florida Rangers, a force of mounted provincials, British Regulars, and Indian allies. On May 17, 1777, a portion of the invading American expedition was attacked by a detachment of British Regulars under Maj. J. M. Prevost assisted by Rangers under Col. Thomas Brown and Indians. The battle took place at a site on Thomas Creek south of its confluence with the Nassau River.

After suffering heavy casualties, the Americans, already discouraged by lack of supplies and the heat, began their retreat from Florida. Only one more unsuccessful invasion of East Florida occurred during the remaining years of the American Revolution.

Fort Tocobaga

In 1567, Spanish explorer Pedro Menendez, the founder of St. Augustine, during his explorations along Florida's Gulf Coast, established a tenuous alliance with the Tocobaga Indians at their principal village on Tampa Bay — Safety Harbor. The Tocobaga Indians rebelled, slaughtered the garrison, and burned the blockhouse.

Fort Tonyn

A Revolutionary War defense erected in 1776 by East Florida's British forces on the St. Marys River near present day Kings Ferry. The fort, named for Patrick Tonyn, the last British governor of Florida, was evacuated and partially destroyed in July 1778 by American troops under General Robert Howe, who took possession the next day.

Vitachuco's Battles

Vitachuco, proud and stubborn chief of the village Ibitachuco, located in the Tampa Bay area, defied Spanish conquistador Hernando DeSoto and his men in 1539. During a feast at DeSoto's camp, the chief and his tribesmen attacked the Spaniards, using pots, clubs, stones, and blazing brands from campfires as weapons. Vitachuco attacked DeSoto and would have beaten him to death, had not soldiers interfered. The assault left DeSoto with a disfigured face and a number of broken teeth, so that for nearly a month the leader was unable to eat solid food. So deadly and persistent were the encounters between the Indians and the Spaniards that before DeSoto departed the area more than 1,300 of Vitachuco's warriors had been slain.

Yemassee Indian Raids

During the late 1600s and early 1700s, the Yemassee Indians were feared as much by other Indian tribes as white men. They were so fierce, powerful and warlike, the very sound of their name was enough to cause panic. Chiefs of the tribe took the name Yemassee for themselves, the better to strike fear into the hearts of their enemies.

The Yemassees, who lived in Georgia and South Carolina, refused to join the union of other Indians in the area that later became known as the Creek Confederacy. Instead, the Yemassees hired themselves out to the British and Spanish as mercenaries — paid Indian soldiers. The British used the Yemassees to attack Spanish settlements in Florida including the villages of the Timucua Indians. In these raids, the Yemassees destroyed a large number of Timucua villages and carried off into slavery many hundreds of Indians.

When the Yemassee Indians weren't fighting for the English or raiding Florida villages to obtain more slaves, they were busy fighting the Creek Indians. Eventually the Yemassees broke with the English and allied themselves with the Spanish. In an agreement with their new friends, the Yemassee Indians were allowed to settle in the deserted Timucua Indian villages they themselves had raided. Following a war between the Yemassee Indians and the Okehumpkee Indians, the remnants of the Yemassee tribe became part of the Seminoles. One of the last great chiefs of this tribe was named Yemassee Mica. He was an ally of Neamathla, chief of the Seminoles, and fought with him during the Indian uprisings in Florida in the early 1800s.

3

Seminole Indian Battles and Forts

Throughout the first half of the nineteenth century, the United States fought a series of bloody and tragic wars against the Seminole Indians in Florida. The first war began in 1817, when President James Monroe gave General Andrew Jackson a free hand to enter the Spanish Floridas in force and stop Seminole raids across the border. Perhaps more compelling reasons for invading Florida included the capture of runaway slaves and the possible seizure of the territory from Spain. The war turned into a search and destroy mission as General Jackson burned Seminole villages and destroyed their crops.

After the acquisition of Florida from Spain in 1821, the United States coerced the Seminoles into signing several treaties, forcing them to give up most, and finally all, of their land in Florida. Faced with death or removal to lands west of the Mississippi, the Seminoles resisted. They were aided by black men and women who had escaped slavery on southern plantations. Beginning in December of 1835, these resolute people fought the U.S. Army in the longest, deadliest, and most expensive of all Indian wars (the Second Seminole War, 1835-1842). Over the course of seven years, the United States sent more than ten thousand regular troops and thirty thousand volunteers into the Florida wilderness to battle the Seminoles and their allies. Casualties were heavy on both sides. By war's end, thousands of Seminoles had been deported to Oklahoma. Only a few hundred escaped capture or death.

A decade passed. Then, in the mid-1850s, in spite of previous agreements, the government sought a final solution to what was considered the Indian problem — the removal of the last Seminoles in Florida. Again the Indians were forced into a war of resistance. This struggle, the Third Seminole War, ended in 1858, with less than 300 Seminoles left in Florida.

At the end of the Third Seminole War, the remaining Seminole Indians either migrated to present day Oklahoma with their leader Billy Bowlegs or remained behind in the Florida Everglades area.

Descendants of the remaining Seminoles still live in Florida and claim the rights of a sovereign nation. Members of the Seminole Nation of Oklahoma are descended from Seminoles expatriated during the war era.

Today, Florida's Seminole and Miccosukee peoples are organized into two federally recognized tribes. Against all odds, these courageous people thrive on seven reservations across the state: Hollywood, Big Cypress, Immokalee, Brighton, Fort Pierce, Tampa, and Miccosukee.

First Seminole War (1817-1818)

Between 1805 and 1816 there was increasing antagonism between white settlers, Florida Indians, and the Creek Confederation near the Georgia/Florida border. The Seminole Indians were harboring runaway slaves who escaped into Spanish Florida from Southern plantations. The United States wished to purchase Florida from Spain, but negotiations had faltered and hostilities gradually became more acute.

Seminole Indian Prisoners. A woodcut showing the capture of Seminole Indian chiefs by U.S. soldiers in the First Seminole War (1817-1818).

Second Seminole War Fort. Between 1835 and 1842 over eighty camps, forts, stockades and blockhouses were built throughout Florida from the south of Apalachicola to every part in the peninsula. Virtually all U.S. Army forts of the Second Seminole War were simple defensive works, often a combination of ditches and embankments of earth and trees to protect relatively small military units for short periods of time.

On November 21, 1817, Brevet Major General Edmund Pendleton Gaines sent 250 men from Fort Scott, in Georgia, to arrest Chief Neamatha at his village, Fowltown. Chief Neamatha had threatened the annihilation of Americans who trespassed on Indian grounds. A gunfight followed and the soldiers destroyed the village — this became the beginning of the First Seminole War.

Indian Attacks

The Indians retaliated for the destruction of Fowltown by attacking plantations and small settlements of the Americans; then they would escape into Spanish held Florida. One of the most shocking massacres was that of Lieutenant Scott and his command. His large open boat was ascending the Apalachicola River with supplies for Fort Scott. In passing a swamp where the Indians were concealed there was a sudden attack, and nearly all on board were killed. General Andrew Jackson, a famous Indian fighter, was ordered to control the Indians and in March of 1818 he started his campaign with a force of 3,500 men, 2,000 of whom were Creek Indian mercenaries.

Jackson Marches onto St. Marks and Pensacola

General Jackson crossed the Florida border and attacked a Spanish fort at St. Marks, which had been occupied by Indians and Blacks. The Indians,

Seminoles Attack a Fort. Seminole warriors attacking a U.S. military post in one of the many skirmishes between the Indians and Government forces during the Second Seminole War.

U.S. Army Soldiers During the Second Seminole War.

however, had learned of the army's presence and had abandoned the fort, allowing General Jackson to capture only an old Scottish trader and two Creek Indian chiefs. The Creek chiefs were executed and General Jackson then marched his troops east to the Suwannee River to attack the village of Chief Boleck. The Indians escaped into the swamp and General Jackson's men captured only two white men who had been living among the Seminoles. The American troops burned the village and then marched back west to attack the Spanish fort at Pensacola. After a three-day battle, the fort was captured and General Jackson returned to the United States with his army. The First Seminole War was over.

After the War

Just one year after General Jackson's invasion of Pensacola, however, Spain signed a treaty ceding Florida to the United States for the sum of five million dollars. The treaty was signed in 1819. Official occupation took place in 1821. Florida was organized as a territory in 1822 and American settlers began moving into Florida in large numbers that same year.

Second Seminole War (1835-1842)

After the First Seminole War ended and Florida had become a United States territory, the question of ownership of the land was still in dispute. The Seminoles considered the 32,286,760 acres comprising Florida to be Seminole territory; the United States government considered it U.S. territory. When the treaty transferring Florida from Spain to the United States was signed, there were approximately 5,000 Seminole Indians in Florida. The uncertainty of their status within the United States was of great concern to the Seminoles, so some of the chiefs made trips to the Indian Agency at St. Augustine to inquire about their rights as residents of the United States territory.

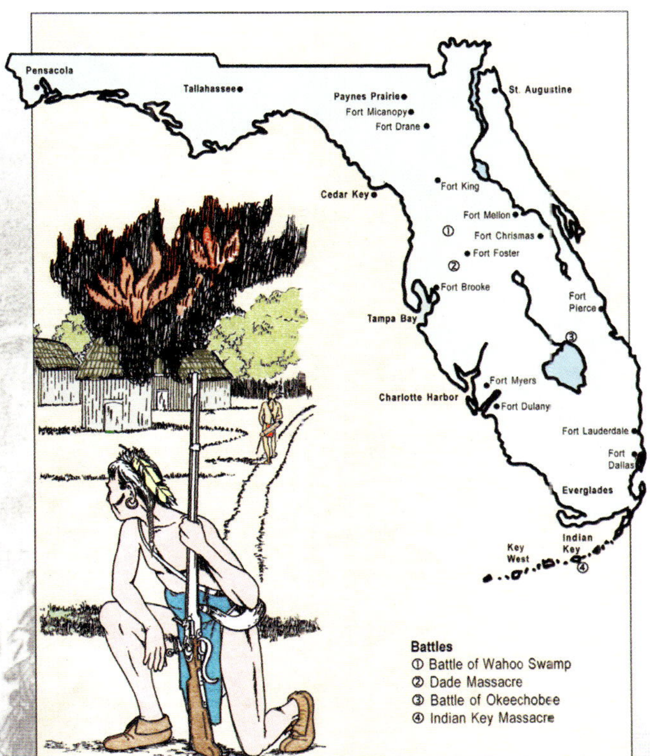

Seminole War Sites.
This map identifies several of the Seminole War battle and fort sites.

Reservation Troubles

The Indians were not satisfied with the lands given them, and would not keep within bounds. As more settlers came into Florida, the white people wanted more land, and plans were made for removing the Indians to lands west of the Mississippi so that all of Florida should be open to white settlers. The Indians simply wanted their homes and their freedom. They did not want to leave Florida.

Treaty of Moultrie Creek

Pressure mounted for the Indians to be either sent west of the Mississippi River or placed in a reduced and restricted area in Florida. Ultimately, on September 18, 1823, the marks of thirty-two Indian chiefs were made on the Treaty of Moultrie Creek, giving up claim to most of Florida with the exception of 4,321,940 acres. Their reservation had no frontage on the Atlantic Ocean or the Gulf of Mexico. In 1824, most of the Florida Indians began their reluctant move into their assigned territory.

Indian Removal Act

Andrew Jackson was elected President of the United States in 1829. Between 1824 and 1829, the true situation of the red men was unbearable. The Treaty of 1823 deprived them of their cultivated fields, plentiful game, and use of either the Atlantic Ocean or the Gulf of Mexico. They were left with the alternative of starving within their geographic limits or leaving their boundaries in order to survive. Friction increased between the Indians and the white settlers and in 1830, Andrew Jackson persuaded Congress to enact the Indian Removal Act, calling for the relocation of all Eastern Indians to the Indian Territory west of the Mississippi River.

Treaty of Payne's Landing

In 1832, the Treaty of Payne's Landing was forced upon the Seminoles; it required all Indians to move from Florida to the Indian Territory within three years, provided, after inspection by a delegation of Seminoles that the western Indian land was found to be satisfactory. In exchange for the Florida land, the Seminoles were to receive lands in Oklahoma, money, blankets, and clothes.

A delegation of seven Seminoles traveled west to inspect the land. The delegation expected to return and discuss their findings with the remainder of the Seminoles before deciding whether the Oklahoma Indian Territory was satisfactory. However, United States agents enticed them to sign a treaty at Fort Gibson in 1833, prior to their return, stating that the land was satisfactory and the Seminoles would move to the land adjacent to Creek Indians in the Indian Territory. There was to be a three-year grace period.

Start of the Second Seminole War

Many Seminoles resisted relocation and deportation efforts. This resistance and the American response became known as the Second Seminole War. In late December 1835, the Seminole Indians had attacked the Indian Agency at Fort King, an Army troop between Fort Brooke and Fort King, and sugar plantations along the Atlantic coast.

Osceola

Osceola's father, William Powell, was an Englishman, who had lived among the Creek Indians in Georgia, and married one of their women. When Osceola was still a child he had come with his mother to join the Seminoles in Florida. When the war began, he

The Seminoles Attack and Massacre Settlers During the Second Seminole War. From an 1836 woodcut.

Second Seminole War Army Fort. A view of a reconstructed Army fort at a popular mid-1900s tourist attraction (Great Masterpiece near Lake Wales) — it was an example of a typical Army stockade used during the Second Seminole War.

was thirty-one years old, and is said to have had a dignified, self-possessed manner, and a frank, pleasing countenance. He was not superstitious as most of the Indians were. He was fearless, but not reckless. He was always kind to his wife and children, and it may have been his affection for them that made him merciful to other women and children. When he went on the warpath, he would say to his warriors: "Spare the women and children. It is not upon them we make war and draw the scalping knife; it is upon men; let us act like men."

Osceola on the Warpath

When no Seminoles had moved west at the end of the appointed grace period, Indian Agent Wiley Thompson forced another treaty upon the Seminoles at Fort King (present day Ocala) in 1835, reconfirming the terms of removal to the West.

Seminole leader Osceola refused to sign the treaty and steadfastly opposed relocating to the West. Osceola organized the many groups of Seminole Indians for resistance to relocation. Rifles and gunpowder were gradually accumulated. Most of the remaining Seminoles banded together in an effort to save their homeland. During the final week of 1835, Osceola and a group of Seminole warriors killed General Wiley Thompson and four other white people at Fort King.

The Dade Massacre

In the latter part of December 1835, Major Francis Dade left Tampa for Fort King with 107 men. He had a six-pound field piece and a wagon with rations for ten days. He had as guide a Negro named Lewis. It is believed that Lewis told the Indians when the march would begin and what the route would be, for they were gathered at the Big Wahoo Swamp to make an attack. The Indians had burned the bridge on the Hillsboro River, and this delayed the expedition a few days.

On the morning of December 28, the same day on which Wiley Thompson was killed, the company was marching along a road near the Withlacoochee River, where the country was covered with palmettos. On the western side of the road, the Indians were concealed in the palmettos, waiting for the approach of the soldiers. A sudden volley from their rifles killed half the command. Major Dade was one of the first that fell. The survivors rallied quickly and drove the Indians over a small ridge. Then they hastily made a small triangular breastwork of pine trees. In about three quarters of an hour the Indians made another attack. Only three of the soldiers escaped. When all had fallen, the Seminoles rushed into the fort, stripping the dead of their arms and accouterments. The Guide had escaped to his Indian friends.

Destruction of Plantations

In late December, King Philip (Emathla) and his son, Coacoochee, led warriors in the destruction of sugar plantations in and around New Symrna on Florida's Atlantic coast. Within days, the Seminoles had destroyed all of the plantations in northeast Florida.

The Battle of the Withlacoochee

Three days later, on the banks of the Withlacoochee River, approximately 250 Seminole Indians, under the direction of Osceola and Alligator, attacked a force of 750 United States soldiers led by General Duncan Lamont Clinch. The soldiers were forced to withdraw because of the large number of casualties. The Second Seminole War suddenly became a serious concern.

Battle at Fort Izard

General Edmond P. Gaines organized 1,100 troops and advanced from Fort Brooke up the Fort King Road through Indian territory, looking for the Indians responsible for the Dade Massacre. Early on the morning of February 28, 1836, adjacent to the north bank of the Withlacoochee River, Gaines' army came upon a shallow crossing. As Lieutenant James F. Izard started to advance across the river, Indian fire began. A lead ball hit Izard in the nose and passed behind his left eye, causing his death.

The Indians attacked from 9 a.m. to 4 p.m. and an order was given to erect a log structure enclosing an area 300 by 500 yards, which was designated as Fort Izard. General Gaines and his soldiers were confined in this fortification for ten days. There were 1,500 Indian warriors surrounding the structure, attacking intermittently. General Gaines was successful in sending a runner back to Fort King asking for reinforcements. This was the only battle in the Second Seminole War in which the whole force of Seminole warriors was involved in a battle. In addition, the major Seminole leaders were present, including Osceola, Jumper, and Alligator. Micanopy was close by for consultation. Later reinforcements for the United States soldiers arrived and the Indians withdrew and dispersed. Five United States soldiers had been killed in battle and forty-six wounded.

Many Failed Battles

The Battle of the Withlacoochee and the Battle at Fort Izard caused the United States' Generals to believe, incorrectly, that the Indians could be repeatedly drawn into conflicts risking large numbers of their warriors. This was not the case, as the Indians learned to disperse in small guerilla bands, attacking when least expected and then disappearing back into the swamps.

Many indecisive battles were fought and many different United States generals were placed in charge of the conflict: Gaines, Clinch, Scott, Jesup, Macomb, Armistead, Worth, and Zachary Taylor all failed in their efforts to bring the Seminoles to unconditional surrender.

Seminole leaders during the Second Seminole War included Alligator, Chittee, Yoholo, Coacoochee (Wildcat), Halleck, Jumper, King Philip (Emathla), Micanopy, Osceola, and Arpeika (Sam Jones).

Fight in the Big Wahoo Swamp

General Thomas Jesup, who had succeeded in compelling the Creek Indians to leave Georgia, was next given the command of the army, but he left the troops for a while with General Richard Call, who was joined by 1,200 Tennesseans under General Armstrong. In November 1836 he crossed the Withlacoochee River and broke up an Indian encampment. He was engaged for several hours with a large force of Indians in the Big Wahoo Swamp. He said this was one of the hardest fights he ever had. The Army troops acted with great courage and coolness. They drove the Indians from the field and pursued them into the swamp until, waist-deep in water, it was impossible for any but the Indians, who were at home in the swamp, to go any farther.

King Philip's Capture

In September 1837, Chief King Philip (Emathla) was captured by General Joseph Martin Hernandez. King Philip sent a message to his son, Coacoochee, begging that he come see him. Coacoochee, when promised he would not be made a prisoner, went to the camp to see his father. He took General Hernandez friendly messages from Osceola and a white plume, which meant a wish for peace.

Osceola Captured

After this Osceola came to the camp near St. Augustine, under a flag of truce. He must have known that his people had no chance of success. After some questions had been asked him, he became silent. Turning to one of his friends, he said in a low voice, "I feel choked; you must speak for me." The talk ended. General Hernandez gave a signal to the troops, who closed in upon the Indians and took them as prisoners to St. Augustine. Osceola was afterwards taken to Fort Moultrie, near Charleston, South Carolina where, on January 20, 1838, almost two years after his victories at Withlacoochee and Fort Izard, he died.

Battle of Okeechobee

In December, 1837, General Zachary Taylor, who had been ordered to find the enemy wherever he could, set out in the direction of Sam Jones' camp with eleven hundred men. He met a large force of Seminoles in a dense hammock near Okeechobee, forty miles west of present day Palm Beach.

As the Indians were protected in front by a swamp, the soldiers were at a disadvantage, but after three hours of hard fighting, the Seminoles were driven from the field. However, the losses were very heavy. This was the last standing battle of the war.

Jumper and Followers Surrender

While General Zachary Taylor was on his march, Jumper and a few families of Indians had come to Tampa and said they were ready to leave Florida. After this, from time to time, small bands would come in, or were captured, and in the spring a party of more than twelve hundred Indians were sent to Oklahoma.

A few weeks later three hundred more were sent. They were very unhappy. No lands had been set apart for them, for it was intended they should join their old enemies, the Creeks. This they were not willing to do. The Cherokees offered them a home on their reservation until lands were set apart for them.

General Macomb's Treaty

General Macomb was sent from Washington to make an agreement with the Indians. He agreed that they should be allowed to remain below Peace River and Lake Okeechobee, and the war was declared ended. This arrangement did more harm than good, for at the very time the army was ordered to cease fighting, the Indians were continuing to destroy life and property, and soon there were more attacks than before in all parts of the Territory. The war was not yet ended.

Seminoles Retreat into the Everglades

General William Jenkins Worth took command in May 1841, and at once sent parties into every swamp and hammock where the Indians might be found. The Indians had scarcely a hope left, but still made their fight, and said they would kill any messenger who came to talk to them about surrender. The Seminoles retreated farther and farther southward into the Everglades.

Coacoochee Deported

A few months before General William Worth had received command of the army, he had sent for Coacoochee to come and have a talk with him. Coacoochee came dressed in a colorful costume that he had gotten from a company of traveling actors attacked near St. Augustine some time before. He promised to bring in his band for emigration, but afterwards said they were scattered and he could not collect them as soon as he had promised. He came to the camp several times afterwards, but said he could not get his band together. Finally Major Childs, believing he did not intend to keep his word, had Coacoochee and the few who were with him, arrested and sent to Indian Territory in the west.

End of the War

After this, other bands surrendered or were captured, and in the spring of 1842, General Worth informed the government that only about three hundred Indians remained in the Territory.

The Second Seminole War was the longest, bloodiest, and most costly Indian War in United States history. The war lasted almost seven years, from 1835 to 1842. For every two Seminole Indians moved to Oklahoma, one American soldier died, with 1,500 killed in battle and many more dead from malaria and other afflictions. An unknown number of white settlers were also killed. The Army had at one time employed nearly 9,000 men against hardly 2,000 Seminole warriors.

In 1842, the United States government decided that the expense of men and money for capturing or killing the remaining Seminoles who were in the Everglades was too great; the government gave up trying to subdue the remaining Seminoles. The Second Seminole War ended with the Seminole Indians never formally being conquered.

Two of the generals, Winfred Scott and Zachary Taylor, were afterwards distinguished in the Mexican War. General Zachary Taylor, after the close of the war, was elected President of the United States, and was called by the Indians "Great Father."

Second Seminole War Reenactments

Each year, at several locations throughout Florida, re-enactors, complete with actual dress and weapons of the period, present authentic re-enactments of skirmishes that took place during the Second Seminole War. Some of the reenactments are:

- Dade Massacre Reenactment at Bushnell
- Dunlawton Plantation Raid Reenactment at Port Orange
- Fort Christmas Reenactment at Christmas
- Fort Cooper Reenactment at Inverness
- Fort Foster Reenactment at Zephyrhills
- Spring Garden Plantation Battle at DeLeon Springs

Second Seminole War (1835-1842). The Second Seminole War was costly to both sides. The ranks of the Indians were decimated and they, in turn, killed about 2,500 soldiers and an unknown number of settlers. In the end, over 4,000 Seminole Indians were relocated to Indian Territory in the west. *(Reenactment photos)*

Fort Brooke. U.S. soldiers at the fort on Tampa Bay around 1837.

Fort Brooke Barracks. Officer quarters at Fort Brooke as they appeared around 1903.

Fort Brooke

Established in 1824 at the head of Tampa Bay, east of the Hillsborough River, the fort was named in honor of Brevet Brigadier General George Mercer Brooks, who entered the Army in 1808 as First Lieutenant in the Fifth Infantry. Fort Brooke was the terminus of the following military roads: northward to Fort King, eastward to Fort Cummings, and thence to Fort Davenport, Fort Gatlin, and Fort Maitland, and eastward to the south to Fort Fraser and Fort Gardner.

Fort Brooke was the most important fort in Florida during the early years of the Second Seminole War and, in 1836, it served as the headquarters for General Edmund Gaines during his Indian campaign. As late as 1841, the garrison's complements aggregated 680 officers and men. Fort Brooke became an embarkation point from which Seminoles were removed westward to Indian Territory. As the fighting shifted to southern Florida, the center of military activity was transferred to Fort Myers.

As Fort Brooke became a major military establishment, the little town of Tampa grew on the outskirts and, during the first three decades of its existence, depended upon the direct and indirect military spending as the chief means of subsistence for its citizens.

Fort Bulow

One of the largest and most prosperous plantations in East Florida was Bulowville, with 300 slaves, 1,200 acres planted in cotton, and 1,000 acres in sugar cane. The grounds consisted of a grand mansion, a stone Sugar Mill, a sawmill, and many other buildings including forty-six houses for slaves. The plantation was started by Charles W. Bulow, who died in 1823, and then run by his son, John.

John Bulow's profitable plantation venture ended with the outbreak of the Second Seminole War. In an effort to protect the plantations south of St. Augustine along the Halifax, Matanzas, and St. Johns rivers, a detachment of Florida Militia, under the command of Major Benjamin Putnam, was sent out from St. Augustine. His objective was to defend the area from Seminole Indians, so he selected a strategic base of operations — Bulowville (also called Fort Bulow).

Around January 31, 1836, the Seminole Indians overran, looted, and burned Bulowville and other plantations in the area. Residents of St. Augustine, forty miles to the north, reported a rosy glow in the sky, which came from the roaring fire at the plantation — the beautiful mansion, large Sugar Mill, and other buildings were all destroyed.

Bulowville Ruins. Sugar Mill ruins are still standing at the former Bulowville plantation site.

Fort Butler

Located on the west bank of the St. Johns River at present day Astor, Fort Butler was built in 1838. It consisted of a crude log stockade and barracks for the garrison. The fort was one of the military installations designed to protect the St. Johns River, which served as an important artery of communication with the garrisons in central Florida. On the opposite side of the river, near the frontier settlement of Volusia, stood Fort Call. In May 1864, Captain John J. Dickison, Confederate leader, and his 2nd Cavalry crossed the St. Johns River and raided Fort Butler, taking eighty-eight infantrymen and six cavalrymen prisoners, with arms and equipment.

Fort Call

This fort was established in December 1836 by Major J. L. Gardner on the St. Johns River near Volusia.

Cape Florida Lighthouse Raid

John W. B. Thompson, keeper of the 95-foot tall Cape Florida Lighthouse, had trouble in the 1800s with hostile Seminole Indians. On July 23, 1836, Thompson glimpsed Indians creeping through the underbrush toward the lighthouse. He locked the lighthouse door just as the Indians attacked. Oil, spilled from the lantern by a rain of bullets, ignited and turned the lighthouse into an inferno. Thompson laid on a platform ninety feet above the ground with two bullets in each foot until men from a passing ship rescued him.

Cape Sable Skirmish

On April 10, 1840, an expedition of Marines and Navy sailors landed on Cape Sable and were attacked by a large force of Seminole Indians. The naval force defended itself for a few hours until rescued — without loss of any of their group.

Fort Carroll

Established in January 1841 on the south shore of Lake Hancock, the post was named in honor of Sergeant Major Francis Carroll, who was killed in December 1840; it was abandoned shortly thereafter.

Fort Casey

Established in January 1850 on the east central Cayo Costa Island near the entrance to Charlotte Harbor, two coconut trees, visible at a great distance, distinguished it from neighboring islands.

Fort Cass

This fort was located on the Suwannee River near White Springs.

Fort Center

A wooden fort located two miles south of Lakeport on the southern bank of Fisheating Creek, near the western extremity of Lake Okeechobee, the fort was established January 25, 1856 and abandoned September 17, 1857.

Central Florida Skirmishes

Two major Army clashes with Seminole Indians in early 1837 were fought in Central Florida — first in the cypress swamps northwest of Lake Tohopekaliga and again on the shores of Lake Monroe.

In pursuit of a band of Seminole warriors, General Thomas S. Jesup assembled about 1,000 soldiers at a site around where Kissimmee's airport is today. On January 26, a daylong battle occurred and ended with the Seminoles disappearing into the fifteen-square-mile Hatcheeluskee swamp. Jesup's soldiers were unsuccessful in following the Indians into the swamp. However, they managed to capture twenty-five Seminoles, supplies, cattle, and horses.

Also in January 1837, Colonel William Selby Harney (later Major General) selected a site on the southern shore of Lake Monroe to establish Camp Monroe. Thousands of soldiers assembled there before being sent out to hunt Seminole Indians as well as to map lakes and inland territory. Before the soldiers arrived, Seminole Chief King Philip (Emathla) had built a village twelve miles east of the fort's location on what is now Lake Harney. King Philip and his son, Coacoochee (Wildcat), a fierce warrior, resented the Army's buildup. On February 8, 1837, more than 200 Seminole warriors led by Chief Philip and Coacoochee attacked the fort. Lieutenant Colonel Alexander Fanning ordered soldiers aboard the steamer Santee anchored nearby in Lake Monroe to fire six-pound rounds from its cannon. Bombarded by fire from the fort and the warship, the Seminoles retreated. The Indians continued to fire from behind trees, but the skirmish ended after three hours. During this battle Captain Charles Mellon and three Seminole warriors were killed; fifteen soldiers and two Seminoles were wounded. Three days later, Fanning renamed Camp Monroe for the slain captain. The settlement that grew up around Fort Mellon years later became Mellonville, now part of Sanford.

After similar encounters with the Indians, General Jesup ordered construction of a series of forts about a day's march from Fort Mellon.

Chekika Indian Raids

A band of about 100 Seminole warriors, led by Chief Chekika, traded and lived peacefully with whites in settlements on the Florida Keys and along the South Florida coastal areas. Then, when U.S. soldiers pursuing northern Seminoles into his territory attacked Chekika's people, he went to war. The results were terrible.

Chekika directed an amphibious assault against a settlement on Indian Key. On August 7, 1840, his party of Indians launched seventeen war canoes against the settlement, traveling over thirty miles of open sea from the mainland to the Key to launch their attack. The Indians killed several people, including renowned botanist Dr. Henry Perrine, and looted and burned many buildings. The attack became known as the Indian Key Massacre.

Chief Chekika plundered and raided the coastal towns he had once traded with in peace and attacked various white settlements on the Keys and in South Florida. In December 1840, Lieutenant Colonel William S. Harney and his troops hounded the chief and his warriors until they were tracked down in their Everglades hideout. There, Chekika was killed and a number of his warriors captured. Chekika's tribe broke up after his death.

Fort Chisholm

This fort was established in 1836 at a site three miles east of where the Fort King Military Road crossed the Tatsala River.

Chittee Yoholo Indian Attacks

Seminole war chief, Chittee Yoholo, opposed removal of the Seminole Indians to the Indian Territory in the West. In the early morning hours of March 29, 1836, he led an attack upon a large force of U.S. troops and their Creek Indian auxiliaries, killing them to the last man. He obtained so many scalps that he became known as the Snake That Makes Noise. He was a great guerilla fighter. One of his tactics was to steal the beef cattle grazing near an army garrison and allow the soldiers to starve. He later, however, was forced to surrender, give up his lands, and move west.

Fort Christmas

On December 25, 1837, a force of 2,000 U.S. Army and the Alabama Volunteers, under the command of Brigadier General Abraham Eustis, arrived at a site twenty miles east of present day Orlando to construct a supply depot that was aptly named Fort Christmas.

A company of about eighty troops remained encamped at the fort. Members of the garrison enjoyed a peaceful tour of duty. On their patrols they searched for Seminoles in the vicinity, however, they encountered few contacts.

As the war progressed, military action moved southward. As a result supply ships had to reroute through Jupiter Inlet. It was no longer timely for ships to

Fort Christmas Museum. The United States Army built Fort Christmas on December 25-27, 1837 during the Second Seminole War. A replica of the fort is a museum operated by the Orange County Parks Department.

Entrance to Fort Christmas. This fort was the site of a stronghold of soldiers and settlers during the Second Seminole War. It was 80-square feet of pine pickets with two substantial blockhouses 20-square feet.

Interior of Fort Christmas.
Many forts were built in Florida at the beginning of the Second Seminole War. A reconstruction of Fort Christmas, shown above, is the typical design of many of the forts constructed during this war. Shown is the blockhouse and an 1836 Mountain Howitzer cannon.

utilize the St. Johns River. For this reason Fort Christmas was abandoned in March 1838. A series of forest fires later totally destroyed the fort. While this simple wooden fortification was short-lived, it gave its name to the town of Christmas, a short distance south of the fort site.

Fort Church

This fort was established in 1836 in Fernandina.

Fort Clarke

An historical marker is located on Newberry Road (State Road 26) at 91st Street in Gainesville. Fort Clarke was established as a U.S. Army post near this site in 1836, primarily for the purpose of providing a safe haven to settlers during the Second Seminole War. The fort is named for Lieutenant Henry Clarke of the 5th Infantry, a soldier who had been killed by the enemy earlier in the conflict.

Coacoochee

Coacoochee (Wildcat) was born in 1807 in the village of Yulaka along the St. Johns River. He would grow up to become a great leader and war chief known to the military as Wildcat. His father was the Miccosukee chief King Philip (Emathla) and his mother was the sister of powerful Micanopy, the head of the Alachua Seminoles. When he was just nineteen, Coacoochee led a band of Seminole warriors and runaway slaves in the Second Seminole War. Coacoochee led several raids until he was captured and exiled to Indian Territory. Coacoochee died in 1857 of smallpox at the age of 49.

Fort Cooper

A Second Seminole War post established just south of present day Inverness. On April 1, 1836 after a failed attempt to "punish and defeat" the Seminole Indians in the Cove of the Withlacoochee (Osceola's main village), General Winfield Scott ordered his forces to march south to Fort Brooke in Tampa. Scott ordered Major Mark Anthony Cooper to stay behind to establish an observation post. Scott promised to return in nine days. Over a sixteen-day period, April 2 through April 16, 380 men of the First Georgia Battalion of Volunteers and a company of artillery constructed and defended a frontier fort on a site overlooking Lake Holathlikaha.

Within three days Seminole leader Osceola had discovered Cooper's forces and set up his own camp on the other side of the lake, just out of rifle range. Major Cooper soon found his forces under constant attack from the Seminoles. The two-week siege of Fort Cooper was the longest continuous battle of General Scott's campaign. The Volunteers were often ordered to charge the woods around the fort to drive out the enemy, never knowing what size force awaited them. The Seminole believed that their hated enemy, General Duncan Clinch, was inside the fort. With insults, the Seminole called for Clinch to come out and fight. They mounted a major attack, with more than 500 braves storming the fort. The Volunteers were able to repulse the attack.

When a relief column arrived on April 18, it found Major Cooper's men tired and hungry. They had suffered one casualty and twenty wounded. It is not known how many casualties the Seminoles sustained.

Coacoochee. The son of King Philip, he was a great leader and war chief during the Second Seminole War.

Pine Pickets Surrounded Fort Cooper. A palisade of pine tree logs surrounded a two-story blockhouse. This hastily constructed stockade withstood a two-week siege by the Seminole Indians in April 1836.

Six-pound Cannon. The troops at Fort Cooper used a six-pound cannon as a defensive weapon against the attacking Seminoles.

Fort Cooper. This is the site of Fort Cooper, which was constructed in April 1836 to protect sick and wounded soldiers at the end of the one-month campaign against the Seminole Indians at the Cove of the Withiacoochee. The high ground overlooking Lake Holathlikaha was selected as a strong defensive position and fresh water could be obtained from the lake. The hastily constructed fort was needed only for temporary protection. The 200-foot square fort provided protection for 380 soldiers until they could be rescued by a relief column sixteen days later.

Fort Crane

Built to protect settlers during the Second Seminole War, the temporary fort, probably named for Lieutenant Colonel Ichabod Crane, was located near the northeast corner of Payne's Prairie near Gainesville. The fort was phased out after the war ended in 1842.

Fort Cross

Established in 1838 by Lieutenant George W. F. Wood at a site just west of the upper reaches of the Withlacoochee River near Brooksville, the fort was abandoned when the war ended in 1842.

Fort Crum

Located near the west end of Payne's Prairie, six miles from Micanopy, on May 24, 1840 all the settlers occupying the fort, except one, were killed by Seminoles.

Fort Cummings

Established in January 1839 on Lake Alfred about sixteen miles southwest of Davenport, the post, named in honor of Colonel Alexander Cummings, was abandoned in March 1841.

Fort Dabney

This fort was established in 1836 on the west bank of the Suwannee River near Suwannee Old Town.

Fort Dade

Built at the point where the road between Fort Brooke (now Tampa) and Fort King (now Ocala) crossed the Withlacoochee River, the fort was established in January 1837 on the left bank of the river and named for Major Francis L. Dade. Fort Dade served for many years as a supply depot and observation post in the heart of the Seminole Indian settlement. It was here on March 6, 1837, that Seminole Chiefs Alligator and Jumper met General Thomas S. Jesup to sign the "Fort Dade Capitulation." The fort was temporarily abandoned for the summer and thereafter intermittently occupied until its final abandonment on November 20, 1849.

Dade Massacre

Minor clashes between whites and Seminoles over cattle, slaves, and land had taken place for decades in Florida. By 1830, these problems strengthened the U.S. Government's rigid Indian removal policy. The policy eventually required that all Seminoles be removed to Indian Territory starting January 1, 1836.

Aware of probable resistance by the Seminoles, military authorities decided to reinforce the small garrison at Fort King (now Ocala), where the Indian agency was

Dade's March to Fort King.

located. Major Francis Langhorne Dade would command the artillery and infantry relief units marching the 100 miles to Fort King from Fort Brooke (Tampa). Unknown to Dade, Seminole warrior Osceola planned to kill General Wiley Thompson, the Indian agent at Fort King, then join Chief Micanopy and Chief Alligator on an assault on Dade's relief column.

For five days, the Seminoles observed the column's progress along the Fort King Military Road. At 8 a.m. on December 28, 1835, with two-thirds of the march behind them, Dade's command had already safely passed the most dangerous ambush points along the road. It was bitterly cold in the wilderness along the military road. The first few days on the trail had been so uneventful that Major Dade told his troops, "Have a glad

heart: our difficulties and dangers are over now, and as soon as we arrive at Fort King, you'll have three days' rest and keep Christmas gaily." Dade was reported to have spoken these words of encouragement to 107 cold and tired soldiers in a pine forest early that morning. He had only moments to live. In less than eight hours, only three men would be left standing. Now in open terrain, Major Dade failed to post his flanking scouts. As a cold rain fell, the men trudged along with great coats covering their muskets and ammunition boxes.

Hidden by pines and palmettos, 180 Seminoles waited. Their initial rifle volley at close range killed or wounded half the command. Dade and Captain Upton S. Fraser were the first to be killed. Three of the six surviving officers were wounded. Captain George W. Gardiner rallied the men and returned fire with the six-pound cannon. As the Seminoles withdrew a short distance, the soldiers hastily built a low log breastwork, cared for the wounded and collected ammunition from the fallen.

The Indians' second attack lasted until about 2 p.m., when all the firing from the breastwork ceased. Most of the command was dead. The Seminoles, followed by their black allies, closed in. Three wounded soldiers — Edwin DeCourey, Joseph Sprague and Ransom Clarke — were overlooked and later escaped. Sprague and Clarke made it to Fort Brooke alive. Dade's black interpreter, Louis Pacheco, was taken captive. The Seminoles, with only three warriors killed and five wounded, retired to Wahoo Swamp to celebrate. This battle helped mark the beginning of the Second Seminole War.

Dade Monument. The dead from Major Dade's detachment were buried on the battlefield, but seven years later, their remains were relocated to National Cemetery in St. Augustine where a memorial now stands.

Dade Massacre. The Second Seminole War began December 28, 1835 when Seminoles led by Alligator Jumper and Micanopy fell on Major Frances L. Dade's command, marching from Fort Brooke to Fort King. Although they had a 6-pound cannon and took shelter in a log breastwork, only three survived. This image is from the original oil painting by Ken Hughs in the collection of the Historical Association of Southern Florida.

Dade Massacre Reenactment Photos.

Built in 1838, today the stone Fort Dallas barracks are located in Lummus Park in downtown Miami.

Fort Dallas

In late 1838, Fort Dallas was established at the mouth of the Miami River (north side) near the site of an old Tequesta Indian midden. This Seminole War Army post was named after a Navy officer, Commodore Alexander J. Dallas, in command of the Navy in Florida waters. The post consisted of several log houses and a stone barracks, and was alternately occupied and abandoned for the next twenty years.

During the Second Seminole War, a number of military expeditions by Army, Navy, and Marine personnel were sent from Fort Dallas into the swamps of the Everglades. Fort Dallas was permanently abandoned in 1858. A hurricane in 1874 destroyed most of the wooden buildings. In 1925 the stone Fort Dallas barracks were moved to Lummus Park. The city of Miami grew from the site of Fort Dallas.

Fort Davenport

This fort was established in 1839 on Reedy Creek opposite the mouth of Davenport Creek.

Fort Defiance

This fort was established in 1836 near Micanopy.

Fort Denaud

Captain B. L. E. Bonneville established Fort Denaud in 1837 as one of a series of posts linking American operations south of Tampa to the East Coast. It was constructed on the south bank of the Caloosahatchee River, 27 miles from Fort Myers, on land owned by Pierre Denaud, a French Indian trader. The fort consisted of tents with a blockhouse in their midst and served as a supply depot for troops in the Lake Okeechobee area. It was utilized intermittently until the Second Seminole War ended in 1842.

Fort Doane

Established in 1841 and located near the Big Cypress Swamp, about six miles west of Immokalee.

Fort Downing

Established in 1840 on the Suwannee River, nine miles from the mouth of the Santa Fe River, by Lieutenant I. P. Graham; Seminole Indians later burned the fort.

Fort Drane

Built on the plantation of Colonel Duncan Lamont Clinch, located about eight miles south of Micanopy, the fort was named in honor of Captain Gustavas S. Drane. It served as district headquarters before being abandoned in June 1836 and was the scene of several battles. Later, in 1836, Osceola and other Seminoles burned the fort and adjacent buildings and occupied the site. During the following October, Tennessee Volunteers ejected the Seminoles and occupied the site.

Fort Dulaney

Established in November 1837 by Captain William Dulaney at Punta Rassa, near the mouth of the Caloosahatchee River, the fort was destroyed by a hurricane in October 1841. In 1856, Fort Dulaney was rebuilt by Captain John McCown and used to track down Seminoles still hiding in the Everglades. The fort was permanently abandoned in mid-1858.

Dunlawton Plantation

In the early 1800s, Dunlawton Plantation, located in present day Port Orange, produced sugar cane and cotton. In the 1830s, fifty-six slaves helped operate a steam-powered Sugar Mill and the plantation became a site of heavy agricultural activity. However, plantation operations were interrupted during the Second Seminole War. In January 1836, all the buildings on the plantation

Dunlawton Plantation Battle Reenactment. On August 24, 2000 there was a historical reenactment of the skirmish between early Florida Militia and Seminole Indians, which occurred January 19, 1836. The Battle of Dunlawton Plantation reenactment was held on the original plantation site in Port Orange. In the background of this reenactment was the ancient Sugar Mill ruins of the Dunlawton Plantation.

were burned and the Sugar Mill was partially destroyed by Seminole Indians.

In 1837, General Joseph M. Hernandez returned to Dunlawton Plantation with 170 Federal troops. Here they captured King Philip (Emathla), a prominent Indian chief whose men had destroyed five sugar plantations in December 1835.

Fort Eagle

This fort was ten miles southeast of Live Oak.

Fort Econfinee

Established by Captain Jacob Brown in March 1840 five miles above the mouth of the Econfinee River, the fort was abandoned two months later.

Fort Fanning

Named for Lieutenant Colonel Alexander Fanning, the fort was established in 1838 on a previous Indian Village site on the Suwannee River. It was abandoned in 1843, and today the resort of Fanning Springs occupies the site.

Fort Florida

Built in 1836 on the east bank of the St. Johns River, just north of Lake Monroe and south of Astor, Fort Florida is more of a depot than a fort. It was designed to assist the garrison at Fort Mellon, the site now within the environs of Sanford, in protecting white settlements along the river against attack by angry Seminole Indians.

Fort Florida.

Fort Floyd

Erected in 1838 near Lake Okeechobee.

Fort Foster

Six miles southwest of Zephyrhills is a plaque commemorating Fort Alabama, which was built in March 1836 as a supply depot and garrisoned with seventy to eighty men. The fort was attacked, destroyed, and abandoned in April 1836.

A second fortification was built on the site of Fort Alabama in December 1836, by Lieutenant Colonel William S. Foster, for whom the new fort was named. The fort was garrisoned with fifty troops, who on several occasions defended the fort against Seminole Indians. On two occasions, the Seminoles tried to storm the fort and burn the bridge over the Hillsborough River. Despite this constant harassment, regularly scheduled convoys deposited arms, ammunition, and rations at the fort. By March 1837, about 200 men were assigned to the post.

Reconstructed Fort Foster. After much research, Fort Foster and the bridge it protected were authentically reconstructed on the original fort site. A nearby Visitor Center contains exhibits interpreting the fort, the Seminoles, and the Second Seminole War.

Six-pound Howitzer Cannon. Fort Foster was armed with a six-pound mountain howitzer cannon that would fire projectiles onto the bridge over the Hillsborough River when under attack by Seminole Indians.

Fort Fowle

Named for Lieutenant Colonel John Fowle, the fort was established in 1839 on the east side of the Ocklawaha River, about three miles east of present day Silver Springs. Its purpose was to guard the bridge constructed by the Army at the crossing now called Sharpe's Ferry.

Fort King Military Road. Fort Foster was located on the Fort King Military Road from Fort Brooke on the Tampa Bay.

Soldier at Fort Foster. On special weekends, the fort is garrisoned by soldiers and the U.S. Army and Militia representatives of the Second Seminole War era. Their uniforms, weapons, and other equipment are authentic replicas of those used during the war.

Inside Fort Foster. This blockhouse was used as a hospital and sleeping quarters.

Fort Fraser

Established in 1837 by Lieutenant Colonel William S. Foster, the fort was named for Captain Upton S. Fraser, who was killed in the Dade Massacre. Located near Lake Hancock, southeast of Plant City, it was built to provide protection for nearby settlers.

Fort Gamble

This fort was established in 1839 on a plantation located thirty miles southeast of Tallahassee.

Fort Gardiner

Established on the Kissimmee River near the northern shores of Lake Okeechobee, the fort, built by General Zachary Taylor in 1837 as a base from which to fight the Indians gathering at the lake, was named for Captain George Washington Gardiner, who was killed in the Dade Massacre in 1835.

Fort Gates

Established in 1835 on the west bank of the St. Johns River, it was located four miles south of the mouth of the Ocklawaha River.

Fort Gatlin

Built in November 1838 on the high ground between Lake Jennie Jewel, Lake Gem Mary, and Lake Gatlin, roughly two miles south of what is today downtown Orlando, the fort was named after Dr. John S. Gatlin, a U.S. Army physician, who was killed in the Dade Massacre in December 1835. Fort Gatlin could only be approached from three directions, thus surprise attacks could easily be repulsed.

Fort Gilleland

Established in 1837 by Brevet Major James A. Ashley in Newnansville, the fort was named for Captain Gilleland, who was killed by Seminole Indians near Itchetucknee Springs while en route from Suwannee to Newnansville.

Fort Green

One of several outposts located along the Peace River during the Third Seminole War, the Hardee County settlement, which grew up around the fort, still bears its name. The fort probably originated as a settler's (James Green's) privately built post.

Halleck Tustenuggee Warriors

An unconquerable Seminole Indian leader, Halleck Tustenuggee boasted that his band had never been subdued by white men. This crafty, fearless, and savage leader kept the country around Fort King, Ocala, Silver Springs, St. Augustine, and Micanopy in constant turmoil. He was feared by U.S. soldiers as well as his own kind. He threatened to kill any Indian who surrendered or talked of giving in to the whites and moving to a reservation in the west. He led his fierce warriors into many battles and raids on the whites.

Fort Halliman

Erected in April 1836 on the Withlacoochee River, twelve miles from its mouth, Captain M. K. Halliman and a garrison of forty troops withstood many attacks from the Seminoles at this fort. Halliman and many of his men were killed.

Fort Hamer

Established in 1849 near Bradenton, four miles east of the Braden River, on the south side of the Manatee River, and named for General Thomas I. Hamer, the fort was a link in a chain of log forts strung across Florida in the 1840s as a boundary line between settlers and Seminole Indians. Soldiers guarded the line, patrolling half the distance from one fort to the next.

Fort Hamilton

This fort was established in August 1841 on the east bank of the Ancilla River.

Fort Hanson

Established in 1840 by Second Lieutenant C. Hanson on Deep Creek, thirteen miles southwest of St. Augustine, the fort was abandoned in August 1841.

Fort Harlee

Established by Major John Harlee in March 1837 on the Santa Fe River near Waldo, the fort was abandoned in November 1838.

Fort Harney

Established by Lieutenant Colonel William Selby Harney in 1839 on the Caloosahatchee River at Harney Point (now the site of the Cape Coral Bridge), a party of 250 Seminoles led by Billy Bowlegs and Chief Chekika attacked and burned the post, killing eighteen of the fort's garrison of thirty troops. The fort was never rebuilt.

Fort Harrel

This fort was established in 1837 at the head of the New River (Acotofia River) near Pinecrest.

Fort Harriet

Established in March 1840 by Captain George C. Hutter on the Ocklockee River about seventeen miles northwest of St. Marks, the fort was abandoned in September 1840.

Fort Harrison

Established in April 1841 as a recuperation center for wounded and malaria-stricken Army troops, the post was named in honor of President William Henry Harrison. Located at a site that is the present-day city of Clearwater, Fort Harrison was abandoned after only six months use.

Fort Harvie

The original name of the post that became Fort Myers, the fort was established in November 1841.

Fort Heileman

Established in 1836 at the junction of the north and south forks of Black Creek, near Middleburg, the fort was named in honor of Lieutenant Colonel Julius F. Heileman, who died of fever June 17, 1836 after fighting at the Battle of Micanopy. Fort Heileman was the quartermaster depot for the Army of the South, as well as being a major military post, arsenal, hospital, rest camp, and haven for refugees. When the War ended, the fort was abandoned.

Fort Hitchepuckasassa

Established in 1839, eleven miles east of Lake Thonotasassa, the fort was named for the Indian village the post occupied, but it was soon renamed Fort Sullivan.

Fort Howell

Erected in 1835 at a site located ten miles east of Everglades City.

Fort Hulbert

Established in February 1840 and named for Lieutenant William Hulbert, who was killed in the war the previous year, the fort was located fifteen miles northwest of Deadman's Bay and three miles from the coast.

Indian Key Massacre

Located on the Atlantic Ocean side of Islamorada, Indian Key is a ten-acre historic site that was occupied by Indians for thousands of years prior to the arrival of the Spanish. This small island, preserved and managed by the Florida Department of Natural Resources, is only accessible by boat.

In the 1830s Dr. Henry Perrine, a renowned botanist, came to Indian Key with his family to conduct experiments in tropical plants and trees. Seminole Indians raided the key on August 7, 1840, killing Dr. Perrine and six others and looting and burning several buildings. Dr. Perrine's wife, son, and daughter escaped by hiding in a turtle crawl under their burning house, standing in water up to their shoulders. Lieutenant Colonel William S. Harney, survivor of a brutal Indian massacre on the Caloosahatchee River, was assigned to catch the Indians who killed Perrine and this he did. On December 4, 1840, in sixteen canoes, Harney and his troops left Fort Dallas, made their way across the Everglades, surprised Seminole Chief Chekika on his island hideout, and killed him. Indian Key subsequently became the site of at least two intermittently occupied Army posts.

Fort Izard

Established in 1836 on the Withlacoochee River about twenty-five miles from its mouth and named in honor of Lieutenant James Farley Izard, the fort was a 250-yard square quadrangle enclosed by log breastworks. A major battle of the war took place at Fort Izard in which Brevet Major General Edward P. Gaines' 1,100 troops fought 1,500 Seminole warriors under leaders Alligator and Osceola.

Fort Jackson

Established in November 1838 by Captain T. I. Alexander, it is twelve miles southwest of Ellaville. Twenty-four years before, in 1814, the site was apparently the location where General Andrew Jackson made peace with the Creek Indians.

Fort Jacksonville

This fort was established in 1836 at a site that is present-day Jacksonville.

Fort Jennings

Located on the Waccasassa River, the fort was named for Lieutenant Henry Jennings, who was killed in the war in 1837.

Fort Jupiter

Located about three miles from the mouth of Jupiter Inlet on the south side of the Jupiter River, the fort was established in 1838 by General Thomas Sidney Jesup (1788-1860), who was wounded there. During that year about 600 Seminole Indians were made prisoners at Fort Jupiter and transferred to Tampa. The fort was abandoned at the conclusion of the Second Seminole War.

Fort Keais

This fort was established in 1838; it was located southwest of Lake Okeechobee, ten miles south of Immokalee, and south of Fort Denaud.

Fort Kemble

Established in 1839 by the United States Navy to protect woodcutters working along the banks of the Miami River, the post, occupied by U.S. Marines, was near the Fort Dallas site, located in present-day downtown Miami.

Key Biscayne Post

This Second Seminole War fort, located on Key Biscayne at Cape Florida, was renamed Fort Bankhead in 1838.

Fort King

Established in 1827, the fort was named in honor of Colonel William King, who commanded the expedition from Black Rock to Canada in 1812. He commanded his regiment in the capture of York (Toronto) in 1813, and was temporarily, in 1818, military and civil governor of Pensacola, during Jackson's invasion of Spanish Florida.

The Fort King site, which is about two miles east of Ocala, was the hub of activity during the Florida Indian uprisings. Outside Fort King's stockade, on December 28, 1835, warriors led by Osceola ambushed and killed Indian Agent General Wiley Thompson and four others. On this same day, troops marching to the fort's relief perished in the Dade Massacre. Fort King, except for brief periods, was occupied from 1832 to March 25, 1843 when it was abandoned. In 1844, after the Second Seminole War ended, Fort King became the temporary seat of newly created Marion County.

Fort King Battle

A battle occurred near Fort King on April 28, 1840. Captain Gabriel Rains had set explosive traps outside of Fort King in retaliation for recent attacks against his soldiers. While checking a device that had exploded the night before, a body of 120 Miccosukee Indians, led by Halleck Tustenuggee, attacked a company of seventeen soldiers. The soldiers were surrounded, but fought their way out in a desperate battle. Captain Rains was severely wounded along with several of his men. Four Indians were killed. Rains became known as the father of land mines.

King Philip

His full name was King Philip Emathla and he was a prominent leader of the Seminole Indians on the St. Johns River in the early 1800s. King Philip's son, known as Coacoochee, or Wildcat, also rose to power as a leader of the more belligerent Seminole faction. King Philip and his son were involved with many of the Northeast Florida plantation skirmishes in 1835 and 1836, including the first Dunlawton Plantation battle. On September 10, 1837, General Joseph M. Hernandez and his troops attacked a band of Seminoles led by King Philip at Dunlawton. King Philip and several of the Indians were captured and sent west to a reservation. He died on June 7, 1838, within fifty miles of reaching his destination, Fort Gibson. He was buried with full military honors, including a salute of 100 guns over his grave.

Fort Kingsbury

Established at the northeast end of Lake Monroe near present-day Enterprise, the fort was named after Lieutenant Charles Kingsbury of the 2nd Dragoons, who fought in the battle of Camp Monroe in February 1837 and later died of fever.

Fort Lane

On November 10, 1837 a detachment of soldiers left Fort Mellon on Lake Monroe and headed south to Lake Harney to build the new fort, Fort Lane. It was built in short order on the west shore of Lake Harney, about ten miles south of Fort Mellon. The post was named in honor of Lieutenant Colonel John F. Lane, who died in 1836.

Fort Lauderdale

On the approximate site of the present day city was a stockade, built by Major William Lauderdale in March 1838. Major Lauderdale conducted several expeditions into the Everglades from this two-story stockade blockhouse before it was abandoned later in the year. The Seminoles then burned the stockade. In February 1839, Captain William C. Davidson built a new fortification a short distance southeast of the first fort site. The second Fort Lauderdale was abandoned in 1842, at the end of the Second Seminole War. The fort and vicinity was settled in 1895, and grew into one of Florida's East Coast playgrounds.

Fort Lawson

Established in 1840 on the St. Marks River south of Tallahassee, the post was named for Surgeon General Thomas Lawson.

Fort Lindsay

This fort was established in 1836 by Colonel William Lindsay on the Withlacoochee River near present-day Brooksville.

Fort Lloyd

This fort was established in 1838 at a site seven miles northeast of Okeechobee and west of Fort Pierce.

Loxahatchee River Battle

The Battle of Loxahatchee River was a lively engagement between U.S. troops and a Seminole Indian band. The battle occurred in January 1838 probably in the area of present day Jonathan Dickison State Park, just north of West Palm Beach.

Fort Lauderdale. Fort Lauderdale's prime importance during the Second Seminole War was as a base for expeditions into the Everglades looking for Seminole Indians.

Fort Macrae (Addison) Blockhouse. During the Second Seminole War many plantations were attacked by Seminole Indians on the warpath. One of these plantations was the Carrickfergus Plantation in central east Florida, and at different times, owned by John Addison and Duncan Macrae. In 1836 the plantation was occupied by Militia, renamed Fort Macrae (also called the Addison Blockhouse), and was involved in a bloody battle with the Seminoles.

Fort Macomb

Established in 1839 on the Suwannee River, the fort was named for General Alexander Macomb.

Fort Macrae

In the early days of the Second Seminole War the Macrae Plantation (formerly part of the Carrickfergus Plantation) and Sugar Mill was destroyed by Indians, and on February 27, 1836, the Carolina Regiment of Volunteers occupied the plantation site and named it Fort Macrae. When the soldiers arrived, the Sugar Mill, dwelling house, kitchen, and other buildings had been destroyed, and the barn was still burning. The volunteers were embroiled in a campaign against the Seminole Indians, who had torched a string of area plantations in December 1835.

The soldiers burned the grass, cut the palmetto and scrub, and removed all objects within rifle range, behind which the Indians could conceal themselves. The troops built a breastwork with dirt and trenches, and used the ruins of the plantation kitchen to build a blockhouse within the fort. The ruins of the Macrae Sugar Mill were about 200 yards from the blockhouse. On March 10, 1836, the Seminole Indians attacked the fort at daylight, and a bloody battle ensued.

Fort Maitland

Built in 1838 by Lt. Colonel Alexander C. W. Fanning on the military road connecting Fort Mellon (Sanford) with Fort Gatlin (Orlando) and used as a stockade, the fort was named in honor of William Seton Maitland (1798-1837), a graduate of West Point. Maitland was severely wounded at Wahoo Swamp on November 21, 1836, which resulted in his untimely death at the age of 39.

Fort Manatee

This fort was located on the south side of Manatee Inlet near Grant's Pass.

Fort Mandarin

In January 1836 many of the plantations on the St. Johns River removed their families to Jacksonville and Mandarin. Many of the plantations were abandoned; the events of the past few months had so alarmed the inhabitants that they had fled for their lives. In the summer of 1836 roving bands of Seminole Indians attacked and plundered settlements along the St. Johns River. Fort Mandarin was established in 1837 by General Thomas S. Jesup on the east bank of the St. Johns River north of present-day Switzerland.

Fort Many

Established in 1841, sixteen miles southeast of Tallahassee, it was named for Colonel James B. Many.

Fort Mason

This fort was established in 1837 on Lake Eustis in central Florida by Major Richard Barnes Mason.

Fort McClintock

Named for Major William McClintock, Fort McClintock was established six miles southwest of Lake Tohopekaliga in central Florida.

Fort McClure

First established in 1838 as Camp Wendell, in 1842 it was renamed Fort McClure in honor of Lieutenant James McClure.

Fort McCoy

This fort was established in 1838 on the west bank of the Ocklawaha River, northeast of Ocala in central Florida. Today, the present town of the same name occupies the site of the fort.

Fort McCrabb

Established in early 1840 on the Suwannee River, Fort McCrabb was located several miles northwest of Fort Fanning.

Fort McNeil

In 1837 a stockade with blockhouses at diagonal corners was constructed and named Fort McNeil in memory of 2nd Lieutenant John Winfield Scott McNeil, USA, who fell gallantly in action near Dunlawton, September 11, 1837. He was the son of General John McNeil, USA, and nephew of Franklin Pierce, 14th President of the United States. Fort McNeil was located on today's State Road 532, in the vicinity of Tosohatchee State Preserve near Orlando.

Fort McRae

Established in early 1838 on the eastern shore of Lake Okeechobee and named for Major Archibald McRae, the fort was also rebuilt and occupied in 1857 during the Third Seminole War. Ruins of its original brick foundation are still visible at low tide.

Fort Mellon

Located on the southwest shore of Lake Monroe, in the present-day city of Sanford, this outpost was originally called Camp Monroe when established in 1836 by Lieutenant Colonel Alexander Fanning. In February 1837 the outpost's name was changed to Fort Mellon in memory of Captain Charles Mellon, killed when a force of more than 300 heavily armed Seminole Indian warriors, under the leadership of Coacoochee (Wildcat), attacked the fort.

Fort Mellon was abandoned in June 1837, on account of the high incidence of sickness among its troops. Indians soon burned the post, whose site became a trading post called Mellonville and later the city of Sanford.

Micanopy

Also known as Hulpeurra Hardjo, a feared Seminole Indian war chief, Micanopy violently opposed the U.S. Government's removal of Seminole Indians to a western location. As one of the most important Seminole chiefs, Micanopy helped lead the fight against U.S. forces in Florida. In 1832 a number of Seminole chiefs agreed to sign the Treaty of Payne's Landing, which allowed the cession of tribal lands to the whites and removal to Indian Territory. Micanopy refused to sign, and he supported younger warriors preparing to resist removal. He participated with Seminole leaders Alligator and Jumper in the attacks of December 28, 1835, when Seminole warriors ambushed a force of U.S. soldiers led by Major Frances L. Dade, who were traveling from Fort Brooke to Fort King. Only three of the U.S. troops survived to tell the tale of what was soon to be known as the "Dade Massacre." In late 1837 Micanopy finally surrendered to U.S. forces. Micanopy signed a treaty and was imprisoned for a time, before finally being allowed to move westward to Indian Territory. He was about sixty years old when he died in 1849.

Fort Micanopy

Originally known as Fort Defiance and located on Lake Micanopy in north central Florida, the fort was established in December 1835 by Florida Militia

Micanopy. The first chief of the Seminole Indians, Micanopy and his people challenged the U.S. Government efforts to remove them from their lands. The resulting Second Seminole War ended with Micanopy's exile to Oklahoma where he died in 1849.

under the command of General Richard Keith Call. The post was temporarily abandoned in August 1836, but was soon reoccupied as Fort Micanopy with a garrison of 140 troops commanded by Brevet Major Levi Whiting.

Fort Micanopy was built in the fashion typical of the period although it was larger than most of the Florida fortifications. It was approximately 250 feet square with a blockhouse at each corner. During the remainder of the War, the outpost strength figures at Fort Micanopy varied from 43 to 432 military personnel until it was again abandoned in February 1843.

Micanopy-Wacahoota Road Attack

On December 28, 1840, Miccosukee Indians under Halleck Tustenuggee and Coosa Tustenuggee attacked an Army escort at Martin's Point on the Micanopy-Wacahoota Road and killed six people, including Mrs. Montgomery, the wife of Lieutenant Alexander Montgomery at Fort Micanopy. The death of Mrs. Montgomery caused outrage over the war in newspapers across the country.

Fort Micanopy.

Fort Mills

This fort was established in 1836 at a site near present-day LaCrosse and named after Colonel William J. Mills.

Fort Moniac

Established in June 1838 on the St. Marys River near the Georgia border, the fort was named for Lieutenant David Moniac, a Creek Indian who was killed in 1836 at the Battle of Wahoo Swamp.

Fort Myers

During the Second Seminole War, a temporary fort was established and named for Lieutenant John Harvie. Fort Harvie was a large stockade with four barracks, eight officer's quarters, administration building, laundry, blacksmith, hospital, bakehouse, storehouses, and wharf. It covered about eight blocks of present-day downtown Fort Myers. Seminoles burned the fort, which was later rebuilt and named Fort Myers.

Fort New Buena Vista

This fort was erected in 1836 near Palatka.

Fort Newnansville

A military post in present-day Alachua County in northeast Florida, the fort was a fortified haven for settlers seeking protection from the Indians during the Second Seminole War. The fort was named for Colonel Daniel Newnan.

Fort New Smyrna

Established in May 1837 by Captain Lucian B. Webster on the site of the former Dunham mansion in New Smyrna, the fort was burned by Indians in 1835 and was one of the staging areas for General Thomas Jesup's 1837-1838 campaign against the Seminoles. The fort was abandoned and rebuilt several times before officially closing November 10, 1853.

Fort New Switzerland

This fort was established on the east bank of the St. Johns River at the present-day town of Switzerland.

Fort Noel

Established in 1839 on the Aucilla River in northern Florida, the fort was named for Captain Thomas Noel whose command built the fort. Fort Noel was abandoned at the conclusion of the war.

Fort Ogden

Named for Captain Edmund Ogden of the 8th U.S. Infantry, the fort was established in July 1841, as an advanced position for the Big Cypress campaign. In addition, fifty-five canoes were constructed for the next winter's Everglades expedition. Before the camp was abandoned in the fall, an influential Indian leader, Coacoochee, visited Fort Ogden. The community of Fort Ogden developed in this citrus and cattle region in the last part of the nineteenth century and took its name from the fort.

Okeechobee Battle

The Battle of Okeechobee was the last major engagement of the Second Seminole War. On Christmas Day, 1837, Colonel Zachary Taylor and over a thousand soldiers battled a Seminole Indian force led by Alligator, Coacoochee (Wildcat), Arpeika (Sam Jones), Otolke-Thloco, and Billy Bowlegs. The encounter took place along the northeastern shore of Lake Okeechobee. This engagement was one of the fiercest of the Second Seminole War and took place in a saw grass marsh. The hand-to-hand encounter lasted three hours. The mounted troops were helpless in this swampy terrain, and the foot soldiers were also handicapped. The Seminoles disappeared into the swamps. The issue remained unsettled, but Colonel Taylor was promoted to Brigadier General for his role in this engagement. During this battle twenty-eight soldiers were killed and 112 wounded; the Seminole Indian toll was eleven killed and fourteen wounded. The Army victory caused a turning point in the war after which no full-scale conflicts occurred and the number of smaller attacks diminished.

Osceola

Probably the best known Seminole Indian — and one of the best known American Indians — was Osceola, who inspired his people to fight the Americans and never surrender their lands. He was a brief shining star of the Seminole resistance and a key leader in the Second Seminole War. His betrayal at the hands of Army soldiers

Osceola's Last Battlefield. A grassy knoll with pine trees on the bank of the Ocklawaha River. About thirty-four miles north of this spot, on the Ocklawaha River, is Payne's Landing, the location where the first treaty with the Seminole Indians was signed in 1832, to be broken by Osceola, the famed war leader, in 1835.

Author's Note: Postcard inscription is wrong — Osceola was never a chief.

Osceola, Seminole Leader. His courage, leadership, and intelligence helped guide the Indians in the Second Seminole War. In 1837, Osceola (shown on the right) was captured and imprisoned at a peace conference while under a flag of truce; he died the following year.

Osceola Being Captured. Disease, poor nutrition, and the scarcity of ammunition eventually led Osceola to truce talks with Army officers. General Joseph Hernandez, acting under orders, seized the famous Seminole leader and seventy of his braves, while assembled under a white flag. They were taken to St. Augustine and imprisoned in Fort Marion (Castillo de San Marcos).

under a flag of truce raised a storm of protest that shook this country and those abroad.

Osceola was a bitter and betrayed man from the time he was first bound with chains at Fort King until he promised to go west with other Seminoles whose lands and cattle were desired by white settlers until the final indignity of his death in a prison cell several years later.

Palm City Depot

Established in 1838 by General Thomas S. Jesup in the vicinity of Palm City, development of the St. Lucie Canal destroyed all traces of the original site.

Peliklakaha Attacks

In March 1836 Brevet Brigadier General Abraham Eustis and his soldiers burned the Seminole Indian village of Peliklakaha. On April 19, 1842, Colonel William Jenkins Worth led an attack on Halleck Tustenuggee's camp at Peliklakaha near Lake Ahapopka (Apopka). Army soldiers took the camp and defending position, but the Indians escaped. One soldier was killed in the battle and was buried in the muck of the surrounding swamp.

Fort Peyton

Named for 1st Lieutenant Richard H. Peyton, the post's commander, the fort was located on Moultrie Creek, a few miles southwest of St. Augustine. On October 20, 1837, Osceola, the great leader of the Seminole Indians, was en route to the fort under the Indian equivalent of a flag of truce when he and other Seminole warriors were captured under the orders of General Thomas S. Jesup. A marker about a mile from the post indicates the site of the betrayal. Fort Peyton was abandoned in 1940.

Fort Pierce

This fort was established in 1838 on the west bank of the Indian River in honor of Brevet Lieutenant Colonel Benjamin Kendrick Pierce, brother of the 14th President of the United States, Franklin Pierce.

Fort Pleasant

Established in 1838 on the Econfinee River, about twenty miles from its mouth, the fort was abandoned after the war ended.

Fort Poinsett

Established in 1836 to protect the Mangrove Coast in southwest Florida and named for Secretary of War Joel R. Poinsett, the post was abandoned in 1843.

Fort Port Leon

Established in 1841 in Port Leon, five miles southeast of St. Marks, the fort was destroyed by a hurricane and tidal wave in 1843.

Fort Preston

This fort was established in 1840 by Captain E.D. Bullock on the left bank of the Apalachicola River, thirteen miles from Aspalaga.

Fort Reid

This fort was established by Lieutenant Colonel William S. Harney in July 1840, about a mile south of Fort Mellon, on Lake Monroe. Mule-team trails were laid out to haul supplies from Fort Mellon to soldiers at Fort Reid. The fort was abandoned at the conclusion of the Second Seminole War in 1842; however, settlers in the area intermittently used it as a defense against Seminole Indian attacks.

Fort Roger Jones

This fort was established in 1839 on the Aucilla River in northwest Florida.

Fort Russell

Established in 1839 on Key Biscayne and named for Captain Samuel Russell, the U.S. Navy occupied the post from 1842-1844.

Fort Sanderson

Established by 2nd Lieutenant C. Hanson, 7th Infantry, in July 1840 in Clay County, the fort was named in memory of Lieutenant James S. Sanderson, 7th Infantry, who was killed by Seminole Indians in May 1840. The fort was abandoned in February 1841.

Fort Searle

This fort was established in 1839 at a site about six miles east of Picolata, as an outlying post of St. Augustine.

Seminole Indian Prisoners at Castillo De San Marcos

Between September 8 and October 27, 1837, the United States Military, under the command of General Joseph M. Hernandez, took nine Seminole leaders, eighty-one warriors, and an unknown number of women and children prisoner. The leaders imprisoned were Miccopotokee, Yuchi Billy, Yuchi Jack, Coacoochee, Osceola, Chittee Yahola, Holata Tustenuggee, Talmus Hadjo, and John Cavallo. About fifteen feet above the floor of the damp cell where Coacoochee, John Cavallo, and Talmus Hadjo were kept with other Seminoles was a tall but narrow window. The window measures about five feet high by nine inches wide on the outside. Through this small opening, on November 29, 1837, during the dark of the moon, they made a daring escape and took with them fifteen warriors and two women.

Fort Shannon

Established in 1838 on the western bank of the St. Johns River at Palatka, the fort was one of the major quartermaster depots in Florida during the Second Seminole War. It operated under Gen. William J. Worth until he assumed command of the armies in Florida. Military facilities included a hospital, barracks, blockhouses, and stables for more than 400 horses. During the fort's existence, Palatka was military in appearance and under military control.

Fort Simmons

Established in 1841 on the south bank of the Caloosahatchee River, six miles below Fort Denaud and forty miles upstream from Fort Dulaney, the fort was abandoned in 1842.

Spring Garden Plantation

In 1836, during the Second Seminole War, Seminole Indians raided the Spring Garden Plantation, located in present-day DeLeon Springs State Recreation Area, destroying it and the Sugar Mill. The Indians enjoyed the hospitality of the spring for two years. General Zachary Taylor, commander of the U.S. Army in Florida, retook the springs from the Seminoles in 1838.

Fort Stanbury

Established in 1839 on the Wakulla River, twelve miles south of Tallahassee, the post was named for General F. E. Stansbury, who distinguished himself in the War of 1812.

Fort Starke

This fort was established in 1840 on an ancient Indian mound at the mouth of the Manatee River near the present-day DeSoto National Memorial in Bradenton.

Fort Sullivan

Established in January 1839, eleven miles east of Lake Thonotassassa, the fort was named in honor of Army surgeon Wade Sullivan who had recently died. It was abandoned in October of the same year. The original name of the stockade was Fort Hitchepuckasassa.

Spring Garden Plantation Reenactment. Each year at DeLeon Springs State Recreation Area near DeLand, there is a historical reenactment of the skirmish between early Florida Militia and Seminole Indians, which occurred in January 1836, at the beginning of the Second Seminole War. An 1836 setting is provided at the site and the re-enactors proceed to simulate the Seminole Indian raid on the Spring Garden Plantation.

Spring Garden Plantation Reenactment. The re-enactors, complete with actual dress and weapons of the period, present an authentic picture of the skirmish. In the background of this reenactment are several old Sugar Mill ruins of the Spring Garden Plantation.

Fort Tarver

This fort was located a few miles southeast of Gainesville on the north side of Payne's Prairie.

Fort Taylor

Established in 1837 by Colonel David E. Twiggs and his troops, the fort, built on the western bank of Lake Winder near an old Indian mound, was used only for a short time as the Seminole Indians moved south toward the Everglades. Fort Taylor was located at the end of the old Military Trail.

Fort Thompson

Located on the Caloosahatchee River, near present-day LaBelle, the fort was named in honor of Lieutenant Colonel Alexander R. Thompson who was killed in the Battle of Okeechobee in December 1837. The fort was reactivated during the Third Seminole War.

Fort Van Courtland

Located at Lake Kingsley in northeast Florida.

Fort Van Swearingen

Named for Captain J. Van Swearingen, who was killed in the Battle of Okeechobee, the post was located six miles northeast of Lake Okeechobee (near Zana), eleven miles southeast of Fort Floyd in Okeechobee, and fourteen miles northwest of Indiantown.

Fort Volusia

This fort was established in February 1836, on a large Indian shell mound on the east bank of the St. Johns River, three miles south of Lake George.

Fort Vose

Named for Lieutenant Josiah H. Vose, Jr., the fort was located about a mile east of the Ancilla River, twenty-four miles from its mouth.

Fort Wacahoota

Established in 1840 in the vicinity of the present-day town, about nine miles southwest of Micanopy, the fort originally had been the site of the Mission Francisco de Potato established in the seventeenth century. The fort was abandoned at the end of the war.

Fort Wacissa

Established in 1838, the fort was located near the junction of the Wacissa and Ancilla rivers.

Wahoo Swamp Battle

Wahoo Swamp is located about midway between the present cities of Tampa and Ocala and surrounds a part of the Ocklawaha River. On November 21, 1836 the Battle of Wahoo Swamp was fought on the east bank of the Withlacoochee River. Indian forces had concentrated in Wahoo Swamp to oppose General (and Territorial Governor) Richard Keith Call's pursuing army. The attack of November 21 began with the advance of a mile-long line of about 2500 men including 1,200 Tennessee Volunteers, regular army artillery and officers, Florida militiamen, and several hundred friendly Creek Indians. In the fierce engagement fought from tree to tree in mud and water, American troops pushed the Seminoles across the slough west of Bushnell. The Indians' return fire resulted in the death of Major David Moniac, a Creek regular army officer who led a bold attack across the swamp. Near nightfall, army commanders decided not to pursue the Indians further due to the seemingly impassable terrain and to the lack of supplies. Army casualties were low; the number of Indian losses remains unknown. Captain William Seton Maitland never recovered from the effects of the wound inflicted by a Seminole warrior in this battle (Fort Maitland was later named in his honor).

Fort Walker

Established in 1838 west of Orange Lake, the post was named for Captain William H. T. Walker.

Fort Ward

This fort was established in 1836 near the present-day town of Providence, on the Santa Fe River.

Warner's Ferry Stockade

A fortified Indian defense established during the Second Seminole War by local plantation owners, the stockade was located on the east side of the Withlacoochee River near Bellville.

Fort Weedman

This fort was established in 1837, about eight miles west of St. Augustine.

Fort Westcott

This Seminole War Army fort was located in the Florida Everglades, near Monroe Station.

Fort Wheelock

Established in 1840, the fort was named for Lieutenant Thompson B. Wheelock and was located on the southwest side of Orange Lake, near Micanopy.

Fort White

This fort was established on the left bank of the Santa Fe River, four miles west of present-day Fort White.

Fort Winder

This fort was located on the Peace River, two miles from Fort Ogden.

Withlacoochee River Battlefields

Several of the decisive battles of the Second Seminole War were fought along the Withlacoochee River. Three days after the Dade Massacre in December 1835, General Duncan L. Clinch, with 280 regular soldiers and 500 militia, was attacked by a Seminole war party at the river just north of the junction of present-day Marion, Sumter, and Citrus counties. The Indians were repulsed, but not defeated.

When news of the fighting reached Army officials, General Edmund F. Gaines and 700 troops were diverted from New Orleans to defend Fort Brooke in Tampa. General Winfield Scott was given command of the armies dispatched to rout the Seminoles. Both generals battled Osceola's forces in the tri-county corner, General Gaines in February 1836 and General Scott the following month, but neither army was able to pursue its quarry into the dense swamps and hammocks of central Florida.

The only other significant encounter in the area occurred in November 1836 when General Richard Keith Call attacked an Indian encampment in the Big Wahoo Swamp, a few miles northeast of the Dade Battlefield. Reinforced by 1,200 troops under General Armstrong, the Army soldiers chased the Seminoles until they were "waist deep" in the swamp and could follow no further.

Fort Wool

This fort was established on the west bank of the Suwannee River, about ten miles from its mouth.

Third Seminole War (1855-1858)

On December 7, 1855, Army surveyor First Lieutenant George L. Hartsuff and his eleven-man crew came across Chief Billy Bowleg's camp in the Big Cypress Swamp and found he was away from home. The surveyors found a garden of bananas, beans, corn, and pumpkins; they took the vegetables and all the ripe fruit and destroyed the rest. Soon Holata Micco, or Billy Bowlegs, returned home. Enraged, he demanded compensation. The soldiers teased and laughed in his face; then they packed up and left Chief Bowlegs with his anger and destroyed garden patch.

On December 20, Chief Bowlegs and some forty Seminole warriors paid a visit to Lieutenant Hartsuff's camp. Completely surprised, two surveyors were killed and Hartsuff and three men seriously wounded. The Army surveyors finally beat off the attack and limped their way to Fort Myers.

Once again, the Seminoles and the Army were at war. For the next three years Florida became a battleground between the outnumbered Seminoles and U.S. troops. The Seminoles struck out in small bands, pillaging, shooting and burning as they went. One band attacked Braden Castle on the Manatee River. With this new outbreak, the Army moved their headquarters from Fort Brooke to Fort Myers.

Although Chief Bowlegs had led the attack against Hartsuff, it was Oscen Tustenuggee, a war leader from a village along Fisheating Creek, who organized many of the early attacks against the whites. In 1856, a wood cutting party from Fort Denaud on the Caloosahatchee River was ambushed and five men killed. The home of Robert Bradley at Darby (near Dade City) was attacked in May 1856 and two children were killed. During the same month, a wagon train en route from Fort Brooke to Fort Fraser was ambushed and three men killed.

A series of battles that brought an end to Oscen Tustenuggee's raids came in June 1856 when Peace River became the scene of conflict. Several raids occurred where several whites and Seminoles, including Oscen Tustenuggee, were killed. In September 1856, Brigadier General William S. Harney was appointed commander of Federal troops. He brought a change in tactics. Boats were used by patrols to penetrate deep into Indian Territory and some Indian prisoners were taken.

The conflict raged on until the Secretary of War was forced publicly to admit in 1857 that the Seminoles had completely baffled the energetic efforts of the United States Army to effect their removal. They could not defeat the Seminoles.

In 1858 hostilities ended. Billy Bowlegs and some warriors agreed to go to Indian Territory in the west, but about 300 Seminoles flatly refused the peace offer and withdrew to the Florida swamps. The children, grandchildren, and great-grandchildren of these Seminoles are the Florida Seminoles of today. Cofeehatco, Billy Bowleg's nephew, was 113 when he died in 1965. Today an estimated 3,000 Seminoles, heirs of those who eluded soldiers in the swamps, live in Florida.

The Third Seminole War (1855-1858) is sometimes called the Billy Bowlegs War.

Chief Billy Bowlegs. After the death of Osceola, Billy Bowlegs, a Seminole war chief, led his tribesmen against the U.S. Government in the Second Seminole War, and again, in 1855-57 during the Third Seminole War.

Seminole Indian Leaders. Billy Bowlegs and Chiefs of the Seminole Indians. Left to right, Bowlegs, Chocote Tustenuggee, Abram, John Jumper, Fasatchee Emanthla, and Sanparkee Yohola.

Braden Castle Ruins — Shelter from the Indians. During Seminole Indian raids early settlers took refuge in the stone Braden Castle. Although only ruins of this old landmark remain, one can still see the loopholes from which they replied to the Indians with the bark of the rifle.

Third Seminole War. In 1855 through 1857, Florida became (for the third time) a battleground between the U.S. Army and Seminole Indians. This period of war was called the Third Seminole War.

Fort Capron

Established in 1850 by Captain Erastus A. Capron on the west side of the Indian River, opposite the St. Lucie inlet, the fort was abandoned in 1858.

Fort Chokonikla

Established on October 26, 1849 at the confluence of Payne's Creek and the Peace River, near Bowling Green, Fort Chokonikla (Indian word for "burned house") was part of a network of stockades constructed to protect inland settlers between Fort Myers and Fort Meade during the Seminole Indian uprisings. This was the first of several built in a chain from the Manatee River to the Indian River. The plan was to attack the Seminoles from the forts and then drive them out of the state. Fort Chokonikla was garrisoned for less than one year. Billy Bowlegs and General Twiggs met at the fort site to discuss moving the Seminoles from Florida. No combat ever took place at the fort site, which was eventually abandoned on July 18, 1850 because of sickness and death within the camp. Today, the Fort Chokonikla site is located within Payne's Creek State Park, with several trails leading to the fort site.

Chokoloskee Battle

The United States Army launched a major offense on Chokoloskee Island in 1857. The Seminole Indians ambushed and killed Captain Parkhill and five volunteers. A statue at the Florida Capitol commemorates the Chokoloskee Battle.

Fort Cross

Established in January 1857 on Cape Sable (Middle Cape) at Palm Point, four miles northwest of Fort Poinsett, the fort was evacuated about six months later.

Camp Daniels

Established in mid-1855 near Fort Myers.

Fort Drum

Established and garrisoned in 1849 on Drum Creek, about twenty miles north of Okeechobee, the Seminole War Army post was intermittently occupied by Army troops until the outbreak of the Civil War in 1861.

Fort Galt

Established in 1857 twenty miles east of Fort Brooke, Fort Galt was named for Captain Patrick Henry Galt.

Fort Hartsuff

The fort, named in honor of Lieutenant George Hartsuff, a topographical engineer, was located on the Peace River on the site of the present-day town of Wauchula. It was part of a line of outposts established between Fort Myers and Fort Meade to defend settlers against the Seminole Indians.

Fort Josephine

This fort was established in 1857 near Lakemont.

Key Largo Post

Erected in 1857, this temporary post was located in Key Largo during the Third Seminole War.

Fort Kissimmee

Established in January 1850 on the Kissimmee River on a site that is now part of the present-day Avon Park Bombing Range, the Army post was used for scouting operations in 1850 and put into service again in 1852 and during the Third Seminole War. The post was permanently abandoned in 1858.

Fort Meade

Established in 1849 on the Peace River near the present-day city of Fort Meade, the fort was named for U.S. Army Lieutenant George Gordon Meade. It was abandoned in 1854 and then reoccupied in 1857 during the Third Seminole War.

Fort Myakka

Brevet Major Gavriel I. Rains established this fort in November 1849 on the Myakka River, near the river head. It was built to protect settlers during the Seminole Indian uprisings. The fort was later abandoned in March 1850.

Fort Myers Guardhouse.
Fort Myers was constructed in 1850 on the same site as the much smaller Fort Harvie, which had been built in 1841. The Third Seminole War swirled around Fort Myers from 1855 to 1857. After Billy Bowlegs, a Seminole Indian leader, surrendered to the Army in Fort Myers, the fort was abandoned.

Fort Myers

Formerly Fort Harvie, this Second Seminole War fort was burned by the Seminoles. It was rebuilt in February 1850 and named Fort Myers, in honor of Lieutenant Abraham Charles Myers. During the last years of the Third Seminole War, there were 835 personnel in residence. The fort was deactivated in 1858.

Payne's Creek Attack

On July 17, 1849, a group of four renegade Indians attacked the store on Payne's Creek, killing two clerks and chasing away the others. This act caused the U.S. Army to reactivate many Florida forts with a threat of another war with the Seminole Indians.

Fort Rough and Ready

Erected in 1856, this Third Seminole War fort was located at Rye on the south side of the Manatee River.

Fort Shackleford

Established in 1855 in the Big Cypress Swamp on the edge of the Everglades, the fort was abandoned and burned by the Seminoles in 1856.

Fort Simon Drum

Established in 1855 near Immokalee and the northeast part of the Everglades, the fort was named for Captain Simon Drum.

Fort Vinton

Supply outposts were needed for field campaigns, and early in April 1839, such a post, called Fort or Post No. 2, was constructed about twenty miles northwest of Fort Pierce. This fortification was abandoned by or before 1842, when hostilities ended. Early in 1850, when another concerted effort to force the remnants of the Seminoles to emigrate got underway, it was reactivated as Fort Vinton. The post was named for Captain John R. Vinton, who had served in the area during the earlier conflict and had died in the Mexican War. Fort Vinton, an outpost of Fort Capron at Indian River Inlet, was soon abandoned and is not known to have played a role in the hostilities of the later 1850s.

Fort Walbach

This post, located near Fort Myers, lasted only six days. It was established December 27, 1856 by Captain Thomas Williams, and named for Colonel Walbach.

Willoughby Tillis Battle

One of the most important battles in the Third Seminole War took place in 1856 on June 14-16, at a point south of Fort Meade when a substantial force of Seminole Indians and militiamen engaged in a conflict which marked the turning point of the war. The Indians circled the log house containing Willoughby Tillis, his wife, three children, and Thomas Underhill. They fired at the openings between the logs, but Tillis and Underwood were able to put up a good defense, killing one Indian. Only one person in the house, a black servant, was wounded during early hours of the encounter and the Seminoles were forced to take their vengeance upon helpless horses, killing several of them. Militiamen from nearby Forts Meade and Fraser reinforced the skirmish and eventually killed several Seminoles including Oscian (Oscen Tustenuggee), the Indian leader. Large detachments of the Florida militia under the leadership of Captain William B. Hooker pursued the retreating Indians but were not able to overtake them.

4

Civil War Battles and Forts

The Civil War was a period of internal conflict for the United States. In 1861 the Civil War began between the United States of America and the Confederate States of America. The war between the North and South lasted four long years, 1861-1865. The Civil War was the most tragic war in American history. The war divided families. Sometimes one brother would join the Confederate army while another would join the Union army.

One of every five participants in the Civil War died in service. While 126,000 Americans died in World War I and 407,000 in World War II, more than 618,000 Americans were victims of the Civil War. The North lost a total of 360,022 men, of whom 67,058 were killed in action and

Civil War Diversion. Whenever there were soldiers in camp, there were card games. Gambling was a favorite pastime. In the face of battle, the decks of cards also came out, with the men risking what little they had on a turn of the card while waiting orders to advance.

Union Artillerymen Repel a Confederate Night Attack.

Field Hospital. Surgeons tend to the wounded in a Civil War field hospital. In addition to military personnel, civilian volunteers provided assistance to injured soldiers.

43,012 died of battle wounds. About 258,000 Southern soldiers died of all causes in the war. Approximately 94,000 of these were battle fatalities. The biggest killer of troops in the 1860s was not bullets and shells but sickness and disease. Some 400,000 men perished from such maladies as chicken pox, diarrhea, dysentery, gangrene, measles, pneumonia, smallpox and typhoid fever.

During the Civil War, Florida was not ravaged as several other southern states were. Indeed, no decisive battles were fought on Florida soil. Union forces occupied many coastal towns and forts, while the interior of the state remained in Confederate hands.

Florida's Contribution in the War

Florida aided the Confederacy in many ways. Florida's seaports were of great value to help in the shipping of goods. Products such as cotton, tobacco, and turpentine were shipped out to trade with Europe for goods needed for warfare. Saltworks on the coast of Florida were needed by the army. Since there was no refrigeration during this time period, salt was used to preserve meats. This enabled the armies to store meat for longer periods of time to use when needed.

Florida supplied the Confederacy with salt, citrus, pork, and especially beef. Cattle were used to provide food for the soldiers. Cowhides were used to make leather goods such as boots, belts and saddles. The fat from the cattle was used for making candles.

About 15,000 Floridians aided the Confederacy; of these men, more than 1,000 were killed in action, 5,000 were wounded, and 5,000 died from disease. There were 1,290 Floridians who joined the Union Army and Navy.

Confederate Artillerymen. Florida supplied the Confederacy with salt, beef, pork and cotton. Tallahassee was the only southern capital east of the Mississippi River to avoid capture during the war, spared by southern victories at Olustee (1864) and Natural Bridge (1865). Shown are Confederate artillerymen.

Salt Production. During the Civil War, Florida produced salt for the Confederacy.

Confederate Cavalry Charge.

Florida's Battlefields

After the Union Navy took over such strong points as Fernandina, Key West, Pensacola, and St. Augustine, most of the armed conflicts in Florida took the form of a number of small engagements and raids by Union warships against such coast towns as Appalachicola, Cedar Key, St. Marks, and Tampa on the west coast and New Smyrna on the east coast. Jacksonville was occupied by Union troops four times during the Civil War.

Florida's Civil War battlefields were confined largely to interior lands, where Union troops marched in search of food. Coastal saltworks were another target. In 1864, at the Battle of Olustee, near Lake City, Union troops tried to cut off northern Florida from food supplies that originated in the south. Union troops marched from Jacksonville toward Tallahassee and met Confederates in a six-hour battle from which the Union retreated. The Confederacy held strong in more cases than not. Another Confederate victory was the Battle at Natural Bridge in March 1865 where troops and civilians of all ages stopped Union forces from capturing Florida's capital, Tallahassee.

Confederate Troops Charge and Attack Northern Soldiers.

New Technology

The Civil War ushered in major changes in military technology. The new rifled cannon easily pierced the stone or brick fort walls even when mounted on ships. Armored ships rendered the smooth bore cannon mounted in Florida's coastal forts ineffective. As a result, all of the pre-Civil War forts were made obsolete almost overnight. Nevertheless, the forts soldiered on for years, often being used as prisons. Fort Jefferson in the Dry Tortugas, Fort Marion (Castillo de San Marcos) in St. Augustine, and Fort Pickens in Pensacola were all used to confine prisoners.

Artillery in Fort Marion. A Civil War era photograph with artillery in Fort Marion (Castillo de San Marcos) and tents on the rampart.

Union Troops Marching Through Fernandina in 1862.
From a drawing in the New York Illustrated News, August 16, 1862.

Gunners at Fort Barrancas. Held by Confederate forces until 1862, Fort Barrancas was then was occupied by a single Union garrison throughout the war.

End of the War—and Beyond

Florida had been successful in fighting throughout the war. However, in April 1865, the war had ended with the North being victorious. The South surrendered after four years of hardship and much human suffering, thus marking the end of another era. On May 10, 1865, Union troops entered Tallahassee to accept the surrender of the Confederate troops. The Civil War had ended and once again the United States flag was raised over Tallahassee, as Florida again became part of the United States.

Before the Civil War, Florida had been well on its way to becoming another of the southern cotton states. Afterward, the lives of many Florida residents changed. The ports of Jacksonville and Pensacola shipped lumber for postwar rebuilding. Those who had been slaves were declared free. Plantation owners tried to regain prewar levels of production by hiring former slaves to raise and pick cotton. However, such arrangements did not work well, and much of the land came under cultivation by tenant farmers and sharecroppers.

Tragedies of War. The loss on both sides of able-bodied men killed outright, mortally wounded, dead of disease, or wounded to incapacity was over one million. One of every five participants in the Civil War died in service.

Civil War Reenactments

At the end of the Civil War, the sound of shots fired had not even died away before the first reenactments of the war were attempted. For the vast majority of the veterans involved, the war had been the highlight and focus of their entire lives and it proved very difficult to let go. Many were eager to tell their stories of campaigns and battles to their long-suffering wives and children. More than one took to open fields to demonstrate their prowess with rifles.

By the turn of the twentieth century, the dwindling ranks of the veterans were being watched by increasing crowds of spectators as they marched in parades, or reenacted parts of famous battles.

Favorite annual Civil War reenactments in Florida are the Battle of Olustee, near Lake City; the Natural Bridge Battle, near Tallahassee; the Brooksville Reenactment, near Bushnell; the Horse Landing Reenactment, south of Palatka; the Yulee Sugar Mill Reenactment, north of Crystal River; the Marianna Battle Reenactment, northwest of Tallahassee; and the Civil War Naval Battle Reenactment in New Smyrna Beach.

Civil War Reenactments. A reenactment is a living history event of some historic battle or event that occurred in Florida's dynamic past. A huge event such as the annual reenactment of the "Battle of Olustee" may draw thousands of participants and even more spectators. Many of the reenactments are held on or near the ground where the real battle took place. Shown are Union reenactors in authentic uniforms and weapons.

Crystal River

Horse Landing

Holly Hill

Brooksville

New Smyrna Beach

Horse Landing

New Smyrna Beach

Brooksville

Fort Cooper

Pierson

Camp Winonat

Natural Bridge

CEDAR KEY POST

This important military station, located on the Gulf of Mexico near Waccasassa Bay, was used by the military from 1839 through the Civil War years.

The Civil War found only about eight to 100 people on the Cedar Keys, which were seized by the Confederates. Union forces shelled the gun emplacements near the lighthouse on Seahorse Key and fired a salvo on Atsena Otie and Way Key, (a cannon ball from Atsena Otie may be seen in the museum). In 1864 the Cedar Keys became a local headquarters for the Union force. A skirmish occurred near where the salt works were located. Although both ends of the Cedar Key railroad were in Union hands, the mainland remained in Confederate control.

Cedar Keys Salt Factory Raids

On October 4 and 6, 1862, a landing party from the Union ship *U.S.S. Somerset* destroyed fifty to sixty boilers near Cedar Key. These boilers were capable of producing 150 bushels of salt a day.

Cedar Keys Skirmish

On February 8, 1865, Union Major Weeks, with 386 troops from the Second Regiment U.S. Colored Troops and the Second Regiment Florida Cavalry moved out of the Cedar Keys and up the east bank of the Suwannee River. Six miles from Cedar Keys they succeeded in capturing three men and four horses, a portion of a cavalry picket of seven men stationed at Yearty's. Arriving at Levyville on February 10, the Union force captured fifty slaves, ten horses, cattle, and a wagon.

On February 13, 1864, Captain John J. Dickison and his cavalry unit encountered the Union troops at Cedar Keys. They recaptured all of the cattle, horses, and wagons, and killed, wounded, or captured seventy Union troops.

FORT CLINCH

In 1842, the United States government purchased a tract of land on the northern end of Amelia Island, at the Florida-Georgia border. A military installation was to be built on the property, to guard the mouth of the St. Mary's River, protect coastal and interior shipping, and defend the deepwater port of Fernandina.

Building the Fort

Construction began in 1847 on Fort Clinch, named in honor of General Duncan Lamont Clinch, one of the Federal officers who captured Fort Gadsden and later helped conclude the Second Seminole War.

The plan of the fort is that of a five-sided truncated hexagon, formed by scarp walls connecting five bastions, or protected gun emplacements. Atop each bastion was to be located an eight-inch Columbiad, or a high-trajectory weapon also used primarily in defense of the fort proper. Within a parallel to the scarp walls were placed high embankments of sand, called ramparts. Original plans called for the mounting of fifty-nine guns, placed upon the ramparts, located behind the parapet walls. These weapons were to furnish the base protection for Cumberland Sound. The interior space surrounded by the ramparts was known as the parade. Here were located the guardhouse, prison, latrines, lumber sheds, bakery, kitchens, blacksmith shop, storehouse, officer's quarters and soldier's barracks. Rainwater was collected for drinking purposes and was stored in several underground cisterns. The fort was designed to be self-sufficient while under siege.

Civil War Skirmish. This *drawing, from Dickison and his men,* was done in 1890.

Fort Clinch. This 1847 fort was one of the numerous forts designed to protect the state's long and vulnerable coastline throughout much of this state's history.

Fort Clinch from the Air. This aerial view shows the remains at Fort Clinch State Park, near Fernandina Beach. After March 3, 1862, Fort Clinch was occupied by Union forces throughout the war.

Ten-Inch Rodman Guns Guarding Cumberland Sound. Fort Clinch occupies a commanding position where the St. Marys River flows between Amelia and Cumberland Islands. The guns are pointed in the direction of Cumberland Island. This spot offers a great view of the sound, the ocean and Cumberland Island, Georgia.

The fort, built of masonry and stone, contained a two-wall system, brick, and earth. Building the fort progressed slowly. By 1860, only two bastions and one-third of the brick wall was completed. The ramparts were in place, the guardhouse and prison finished. The lumber sheds, storehouse, and kitchens were in various stages of completion. Not a single cannon had been placed in position.

Fort Clinch Parade Ground. Scene shows remains of buildings and parade grounds. A truly historical site, offering adventure and rarely seen ruins of the past.

During the Civil War

With no federal garrison present, Confederate militia quietly took control of the fort at the beginning of the Civil War, in 1861. They did no work on the fort, but rather established batteries in the fort, the town of Fernandina, and strategic locations on Amelia and Cumberland Islands. Union forces advancing along several South Carolina and Georgia coastal islands in early 1862 caused General Robert E. Lee to authorize a withdrawal from the area. On March 3, the evacuation was completed, even as federal gunboats and troops arrived to reestablish Union control of Fort Clinch. Union troops remained in control of the fort throughout the rest of the war. It was during the period of occupation by Union forces that the greatest progress was made toward completion of this huge complex. Working primarily with red brick, the 1st New York Volunteer Engineers expanded Fort Clinch into the imposing structure that exists today. In only

Rodman Guns. View of the terreplein with 10-inch Rodman guns.

Inside Fort Clinch. Inside the walls of Fort Clinch showing Civil War era guns and the parade ground.

five years they completed all five bastions, the walls, prison, guardhouse, ramps, sleeping quarters, bakery, blacksmith shop, kitchens, lumber shed, and storehouse. In 1867 work at the fort was halted and the post deactivated.

Coastal Blockade

The Union blockade of the Florida coasts began in June of 1861. Some blockading ships had regular stations, while others patrolled sections of the coastal waters. The East Gulf Blockading Squadron (EGBS) captured 283 blockade-runners during the war, however, many other vessels slipped in and out of Florida's bays and rivers with arms and goods for the Confederacy. Occasionally, the Union ships would land a party to raid a town. The blockading ships also took off contrabands, or runaway slaves, many of which served on Union ships.

Camp Cobb

This Confederate Civil War post was named in honor of Brigadier General Howell Cobb and located at Quincy in northwest Florida.

Alfred Holt Colquitt

Brigadier General Alfred Holt Colquitt commanded a brigade of Georgia troops in the Battle of Olustee where he rendered distinguished service in defeating the Union Army with little loss to his command. Colquitt's troops were the most experienced troops available to General Joseph Finegan in this battle. The arrival of Colquitt's Brigade was a welcome addition to the Confederate force, and in the Olustee battle they proved their fighting ability. After the Civil War, he was elected Governor of Georgia (1876) and to the United States Senate (1894).

Columbine

Three miles north of Welaka is Horse Landing on the west side of the St. Johns River. At Horse Landing, in May 1864, Confederate cavalry under the command of Captain John J. Dickison sank a Union side-wheel tug, the *U.S.S. Columbine*. The 117-foot long wooden vessel, which drew six feet of water, was to be used by Union troops to tow coal vessels, patrol the St. Johns River, attack Confederate ships, and transport troops and supplies. This is the only incident in recorded U.S. history where cavalry destroyed a gunboat.

Capture of Union Gunboat. During the 1864 Union occupation of Jacksonville, several gunboats operated on the St. Johns River. During one of its forays upstream, the gunboat *USS Columbine* was attacked from the shore near Horse Landing by Confederate forces.

Confederate States of America

The states that seceded from the United States to form the Confederacy were: Alabama, Arkansas, Florida, Georgia, Louisiana, Mississippi, North Carolina, South Carolina, Tennessee, Texas, and Virginia. Confederate governments were established in the border states of Kentucky and Missouri; although officially members of the Union, they also sent delegates to the Confederate Congress. Therefore the Confederate flag had thirteen stars. The Confederate government was established in February 1861.

Crystal River Civil War Reenactment

Rebels and Yanks coexist peacefully in their respective authentic encampments until they suit up for the Battle of the Yulee Sugar Mill at the annual reenactment of the Civil War near Crystal River. Battle flags clash with Union banners on a large site seven miles north of Crystal River on U.S. Highway 19, as thousands of spectators, watch from the sidelines. Scores of infantrymen, artillery units and cavalry riders fight as their ancestors did in the 1800s. All re-enactors volunteer their own time, equipment, and traveling expense to make re-enactment events true

Battle of Yulee Sugar Mill Reenactment.

depictions of the Civil War era, transporting tenting and cooking equipment, uniforms, muskets, cannons, horses, and other necessities for camp life. The event, one of the largest reenactments in Florida, is hosted each year by the Nature Coast Civil War Reenactment Committee. This is a living history example of how men and women participated in some of America's bloodiest battles.

Camp Dickison

This Civil War Confederate post was established in 1864 by Captain John J. Dickison as a headquarters for his Second Florida Cavalry. It was located at Waldo, north of Gainesville.

Dickison's Skirmishes

Colonel John Jackson Dickison (better known as Captain J. J. Dickison), of Civil War days, was the scourge of Union troops on the St. Johns and Ocklawaha Rivers. He deployed his daring little band with such military finesse that his exploits brought admiration by both southern and northern military men.

Dickison and his men had a skirmish at Volusia Landing in 1863. During the following year this small Cavalry troop encountered Union forces near Haw Creek and at Braddock Farm near the Putnam/Volusia County line.

Dickison is best remembered today as leader of the only cavalry troop ever to capture a U.S. Naval vessel. This was the *Columbine*, a Union gunboat carrying two 32-pound rifle guns and 148 men. Of that number sixty-six

Battle of Yulee Sugar Mill Reenactment.

Crossing the St. Johns River.
Captain John J. Dickison and his cavalry recrossing the St. Johns River with prisoners, wagons, and other captured goods.

Union forces were captured, the rest killed or drowned. Also captured were sixty-five stands of arms and three stand of colors. Dickison did not lose a single one of his men. To prevent Union forces from regaining the gunboat, she was burned and sunk.

Days later, at Palatka, Dickison and thirty troops pushed an invading 280-man Union battalion six miles back to the St. Johns River, with casualties amounting to seventy-two on the Union side and only two on the Confederate side.

Dickison was a middle-aged, well-to-do plantation owner at Orange Springs when the Civil War broke out, but he answered the call to arms at once, organizing a Cavalry unit. At the height of the conflict, he and his men were charged with defending the entire west bank of the St. Johns River — the gateway to the interior of the state.

Held at bay on the St. Johns and Ocklawaha Rivers, Union troops tried by land to get into the interior through Gainesville and a major pitched battle occurred there with Dickison and his men again victorious. Guerrilla raids, surprise attacks and ambushes harassed the Union forces from the interior to the outskirts of St. Augustine and Jacksonville.

The Union Army held the east side of the St. Johns River in a firm grip. There were no bridges and boats were kept off the west banks, but Dickison's troops crossed the river at-will on a hastily improvised flatboat that Dickison kept hidden in river swamps. The boat would hold only twelve men and their mounts so crossings took all night and most of the morning as a rule. His raids often netted more prisoners than he had men under his command.

In a night raid at Palatka, a Confederate detachment captured a Union picket of eight men and horses. At dawn a few days later the Confederates surprised a Union company of sixty-five men at Welaka on the east side of the St. Johns River. All were taken prisoner without firing a shot.

One of Dickison's brightest victories, August 2, 1864, turned to ashes when his only son, Sergeant Charles Dickison, was killed in the last volley of shots fired by Union troops as they evacuated Palatka. This was the only Confederate casualty. Despite the crushing loss of this son, Dickison continued his fearless protection of the Florida interior. He received his commission to Colonel in May 1865, just a few days after the forced surrender of all Confederate troops.

Dickison returned to his home near Ocala when the war was over. In 1899 he wrote the Florida volume of *Confederate Military History*, a reference book about Florida's Civil War period. He died at his home in 1902 and was buried in Evergreen Cemetery in Jacksonville.

Camp Finegan

This temporary Confederate outpost, west of Jacksonville, was one of the first obstacles that General Truman A. Seymour's Union force encountered on their path to engage Brigadier General Joseph Finegan's troops at Olustee.

Battle Near Palatka. Captain John J. Dickison bearing the body of his son from the battlefield during a fight near Palatka.

Florida, CSS

During the Civil War, the *CSS Florida* was a successful commerce raider, seizing or burning many Union ships. Under the command of Captain John Maffit, the *Florida* captured or destroyed twenty-three ships during a seven-month cruise. The *Florida* destroyed another thirteen vessels under its second master, Captain Charles Morris. The *Florida* sank after colliding with a U.S. Army transport.

Fort Florida

Built in 1836 on the St. Johns River between Lake Monroe and Astor; during the Civil War, a cable was strung across the river at the fort to impede Union gunboat flotillas. It worked well.

Florida Troops in the Civil War

In 1860 Florida boasted a population of 78,686 free citizens and 61,753 slaves, the smallest population by far of any of the soon-to-be Confederate states. More than 15,000 Confederate troops would come from Florida, most of which left the state by mid-1862, contrasted with about 14,000 registered voters in the entire state. One in eleven people served; one-third of those did not return. About 6,000 of these soldiers died in action or as a result of disease during the war. Another 5,000 soldiers from Florida were wounded during the War.

Gainesville Battle

This battle was fought in Gainesville August 17, 1864, when about 300 occupying Union troops were attacked by Florida Cavalry under Captain John J. Dickison. The Union troops were driven from the city after a brisk fight and suffered severe casualties during hard pursuit, which ended in victory for the Confederate force.

Green Cove Springs

Union troops frequently skirmished with Confederate forces in the vicinity of Green Cove Springs, and finally occupied the town in 1864.

Horse Landing Battle

During the Civil War, the St. Johns River was the principal dividing line between Union and Confederate held territories; the Union troops controlling the east bank and north to Jacksonville and the Confederates the west and southern region. Though the Confederates carried on successful raids on both sides of the river, the Union forces pretty well controlled the river itself. Their gunboats patrolled the river from Jacksonville to Lake

Living History Event. Thousands of visitors attend the annual reenactment of this battle near the Horse Landing site on the St. Johns River.

George, a distance of some eighty miles. To successfully harass the Union troops, Confederate Captain John J. Dickison's raids took place at night, crossing the river in small flat-bottom boats or rafts, usually in the neighborhood of Palatka, which was thirty-five miles from his base at Waldo.

In May 1864, the Union commander at St. Augustine sent two gunboats, *U.S.S. Columbine* and *U.S.S. Ottawa*, and transports with 600 troops upriver to capture Dickison and his Confederate guerrillas.

Dickison's command consisted of approximately 100 of his cavalry company, augmented by an artillery detachment of twenty-five men and two field pieces. When the gunboats appeared, Dickison and his men watched from cover while the 133-ton gunship *U.S.S. Columbine* proceeded on downriver. They then shelled the Ottawa, armed with fifty-two guns, until it hauled anchor and retreated from Brown's Landing south of Palatka.

Then the Confederate troops lay in ambush at Horse Landing until the *U.S.S. Columbine* returned. Some of the confederate force manned two small cannons while others concealed themselves in trees overlooking the river.

One of Dickison's first shells ripped the gunboat's wheel and it ran aground. Although heavily outnumbered, the Confederate unit captured the vessel and burned it. It was reported Union forces lost ninety-one men in the clash, with twenty killed, sixty-five taken prisoner, and six wounded. The Confederate Cavalry suffered no casualties. This capture is the only known event in U.S. history where a Cavalry unit sank an enemy ship.

All that remains of the historic Battle of Horse Landing are two old shells in a Confederate memorial on the courthouse lawn at Palatka.

Every year, more than 1,500 people participate in the reenactment of the Civil War Battle at Horse Landing to honor Confederate Captain John J. Dickison's victorious battle and capture of the Union gunboat, the *U.S.S. Columbine*. The reenactment battle is presented at the Rodeheaver Boys Ranch, a site on the St. Johns River about twenty miles south of Palatka.

Fort Houston

This Confederate defense site was erected in 1865 to defend Tallahassee.

Jacksonville During the Civil War

During the Civil War, Jacksonville was occupied four different times by Union forces between 1862 and the end of the war in 1865. A chain of breastworks, supported by several batteries, was constructed in Jacksonville. In addition, Yellow Bluff Fort on the St. Johns River was fortified; Fort Steele was constructed a mile east of Mayport; a fort was built at St. Johns Bluff, five miles east of New Berlin; breastworks were established on Talbot Island; and two forts were built within the city, Fort Higginson, named for Colonel T. W. Higginson and Fort Montgomery, named for Colonel James Montgomery. Late in the war, Confederate forces established a heavily fortified encampment at McGirt's Creek about twelve miles west of Jacksonville and called it Camp Milton in honor of Florida's Civil War governor. In 1864 there were about 12,000 Union troops in Jacksonville, which included six Negro regiments. By the end of the war, Jacksonville was nearly devastated, having been sacked and burned by both Union and Confederate armies.

Union Soldiers on the Street in Jacksonville in 1865.

Key West During the Civil War

Because of its early occupation by Union forces, Key West, Florida's second largest city, became the only city in Florida under Union rule throughout the entire war. Tropical diseases like cholera, malaria, and yellow fever ravaged the troops. They didn't have natural resistance against these diseases as the natives did.

Bigger than any other fort in the Western Hemisphere, Fort Jefferson, located sixty-eight miles west of Key West, provided the Union a perfect base for the naval blockade. In 1862 the Union blockading squadrons sent raiders inland to burn plantations, recruit slaves for the Union Army, and wreck salt-making operations. During the war, the Union captured hundreds of small blockade-runners, mostly sailboats. The captured ships were either destroyed or went to auction. Their crews were sent to prison or released on parole.

Camp Langford

This Confederate post, located near Jacksonville, was intermittently used as a base of operations by Captain John J. Dickison.

Camp Lincoln

This Union cantonment was established in December 1861, on the western end of Santa Rosa Island, near Pensacola.

Fort Magnolia

This Union Army post was established by Brigadier General J. P. Hatch at Magnolia Point on the west bank of the St. Johns River just north of Green Cove Springs.

Maple Leaf

This Union ship sank off Mandarin Point in the St. Johns River in 1864 after hitting a Confederate mine. The 173-foot vessel rests in twenty-six feet of water and divers have recovered many preserved artifacts from its 400 tons of cargo. These artifacts represent one of the largest discoveries of Civil War era articles ever found. St. Johns River mud, because it contains no oxygen, is one of the finest preservatives known. An exhibit at the Museum of Science and History in Jacksonville shows some of the items that divers have recovered from the ship.

Marianna Battlefield

On September 27, 1864, General Alexander Asboth's force of 700 Union cavalry from Pensacola arrived in the Marianna area to forage and secure Negro recruits. Confederate forces of a few hundred home guardsmen barricaded the streets of Marianna and withstood the first assault. Once the fighting ended, Asboth's troops were said to have looted the town, taking all slaves, wagons, carts, provisions, 200 cattle, 400 horses, and eighty-one prisoners. St. Lukes Episcopal Church, situated in the middle of the battle, was burned. Even though the Confederates lost the battle, they celebrated a victory; a small force of old men, young boys and wounded soldiers stopped the Union troops from advancing to Tallahassee. Statistics vary as to the number killed or wounded during the Battle of Marianna. The battle is reenacted each October. A monument in Confederate Park commemorates the defense of the town.

Marion Dragoons

This elite Confederate cavalry unit formed by Captain William Owens was stationed at Fernandina and guarded the Atlantic Coast from St. Marys River on the north to the St. Johns River on the south. This was a fighting unit so outstanding that it received the highest praise early in the Civil War from then Colonel Robert E. Lee, who was inspecting fortifications along the Florida coast. He called the Dragoons "the finest and most superbly mounted" company he had seen. After two years of warfare on the Atlantic coast, Captain Owen's health failed and he had to retire. The Dragoons were then reorganized as two commands.

Martello Towers

At the beginning of the Civil War, the government fortified Key West with two Martello Towers to protect Fort Zachary Taylor from Confederate attack. Fort Taylor, lying at the entrance to Key West harbor, was begun in 1845, but the Martello Towers were not begun until 1862. The purpose of the towers, East Martello and West Martello, was to fortify Fort Taylor from an attack by land from the rear.

The two towers were identical in plan and consisted of an outer wall of casemates that was designed to carry 10-inch

East Martello Tower. A postcard view of a Key West fort that was built to protect Fort Zachary Taylor from an attack by land from the rear. It was abandoned in 1873.

Entrance to the West Martello Tower. The tower was abandoned in 1866 and is now a botanical garden.

Entrance to East Martello Tower. Today the East Martello Tower is in excellent state of repair and is used as an art gallery and local history museum.

Rodman smoothbore cannons. Within the walls was a tower, a square brick affair with gun slits and cannon firing positions in which there were 8-inch Columbiad cannons. Four rifled Parrot guns were to be mounted on top of the towers.

The term "Martello Tower" has long been used to designate masonry forts built chiefly on seacoasts, generally with thick walls and entrances high off the ground.

The towers were built of brick with arched casemate batteries to the sea and a center tower and galleries, or storerooms, on the land side.

In 1866, orders were received to suspend work on the towers. They were never completed or armed, because the structures proved obsolete when the new rifled artillery came into use during the Civil War. The citadel of the East Martello Tower, with its 8'4"-thick walls on the seaward side, remains one of the best preserved Civil War fortifications in the United States. The present entrance to the East Tower was built in 1854, but originally the only access to the fort was over the rampart and across a drawbridge, entering the citadel at the second floor level. Inside were ammunition, storage vaults, water cistern, fireplace, and other facilities for withstanding a siege.

Fort McClellan

This Union defense fort was erected in 1862 in Pensacola.

Fort McRee

Built shortly after Fort Pickens to protect the opposite side of the entrance to Pensacola Harbor, the fort was named in honor of Lieutenant Colonel William McRee, United States Army Engineers.

Fort McRee was a long rectangle with rounded ends "folded in the middle." This gave two long seacoast fronts, two rounded land-defense ends, and two obliquely angled gorge walls. The sally port was at the junction of these gorge walls. The large casemates of Fort McRee were designed to hold four cannon on two tiers. The division of the tiers was by a heavy-beamed wooden floor. Above these casemates was a barbette tier of cannon.

The fort was designed to be very heavily armed for its size. Forty-four seacoast cannon could have been mounted on the two fronts of the fort, with an additional twenty-four heavy guns on the barbette. The curved ends of the fort had provision for an additional twelve guns each, with fourteen embrasures facing the gorge. The barbette tier of the ends and gorge could mount additional cannon for land defense. Hotshot furnaces were located on the parade in the center of each seacoast front.

Fort McRee. In the years following the Civil War, Fort McRee gradually disappeared as the sea ate away the beach, undermining the fort. By the twentieth century there was only a small part of the fort left. Confederate soldiers were stationed there in 1861 and, as the image shows, the lack of uniforms was not unusual.

The fort was seized by Florida and Alabama troops on January 21, 1861, prior to the actual outbreak of the Civil War. Fort McRee was partially destroyed on November 22, 1861 during an engagement with Union troops at Fort Pickens. The Confederate troops abandoned the fort in May 1862. A combination of the cannon fire against the fort's walls, and the burning of the timber inside the fort caused the loss of structural integrity. The forces of nature finished the demolition begun by Union cannon.

Camp Milton

This Confederate camp was established in 1862 on McGirt's Creek, a few miles east of Jacksonville and named for Florida's governor John Milton. Union troops from Jacksonville destroyed the camp in July 1864.

Fort Montgomery

This temporary Union post was established in March 1863 in downtown Jacksonville and named for Captain James Montgomery.

Fort Myers Attack

Fort Myers Historical Marker. Fort Myers would once again see service near the end of the Civil War. Union forces re-established Fort Myers in 1863 to stage raids on the Florida cattle industry, which supplied beef to the Confederate armies.

In December 1863, the Army post of Fort Myers, inactive since 1858, was reoccupied. The fort served as a supply depot for the Union blockade squadron. Troops from the fort often raided Confederate supply depots in the state's interior, since Florida beef fed the Confederate Army. To discourage these raids, Confederate Major William Footman led 275 men of Florida's "Cow Cavalry" from Fort Thompson (LaBelle) to the very gates of Fort Myers. Shortly after noon of February 20, 1865, Major Footman approached the fort under a flag of truce and gave the Union troops twenty minutes to surrender. After Captain James Doyle, commander of the garrison that consisted of the Union 2nd Florida Cavalry, the 110th New York Infantry, and the 2nd U.S. Colored Infantry, refused, the Confederates bombarded the fort with their field piece. They were answered by Fort Myers' three cannons. The cannonade and musketry continued until after nightfall, when Footman and his Confederates withdrew under cover of darkness.

Nassau Battery

This temporary Confederate defense was located at Fernandina on Amelia Island.

Conflict at Natural Bridge

The Union Army had more than once attempted to reach the interior of Florida. In February 1865, a party of 700 troops started from Cedar Keys, but was repulsed by Captain John J. Dickison. Another expedition was planned for the purpose of taking Tallahassee and cutting off from the Confederacy the supplies from middle Florida. General John Newton, a Union officer, commanded this expedition. He had a large force and every reason to expect success. His plan was to sail from Cedar Keys to St. Marks and ascend the river. St. Marks and Newport were important shipping towns and were located near Tallahassee, the state capital.

Between March 1 and 3, 1865, a Union flotilla arrived in Apalachee Bay. General John Newton and Naval Commander William Gibson had a joint assault plan in mind to cripple Confederate forces. On March 3, 300 seamen surprised Confederate pickets and captured the East River Bridge, four miles north of the St. Marks lighthouse. The following day, Navy gunboats commanded by Gibson ran aground in the shallow waters of the St. Marks River. Gibson spent the next two days desperately trying to get upstream to Port Leon but was unsuccessful.

Gibson's unexpected delay provided just enough time for a Confederate messenger to travel to Tallahassee and warn the citizens of the danger to the Capital caused by the Union landing. In an effort to defend the Capital, every man and boy who could bear arms volunteered to join the thin ranks of the Confederate Army. The forces were made up of wounded Confederate soldiers home to recuperate, men as old as 70, and cadets as young as 12 from West Florida Seminary (now Florida State University). The Confederate troops, commanded by General William Miller, were taken to Newport to prepare a defense.

Battle of Natural Bridge. In 1865, Confederate troops inflicted heavy casualties on the Union Army in a successful defense of Tallahassee, the only uncaptured capital of a Southern state east of the Mississippi River.

On March 5, Union General Newton, with about 600 troops from the Second and Ninety-Ninth U.S. Colored Infantry Regiments, advanced past the East River Bridge, causing Confederate troops from the Fifth Cavalry to withdraw to the Newport Bridge on the St. Marks River. The Confederate cavalry was joined by the volunteers from Tallahassee, where they gained enough strength to force Newton to take a round about route to Natural Bridge. Miller, who had second-guessed Newton's attempted surprise crossing, sent Confederate forces under Lieutenant Colonel George Scott on an overnight march to defend the crossing. The Confederate troops continued to arrive by horse and foot throughout the night. Some reached the west side of Natural Bridge just as the Confederate pickets were engaging the Union troops. The firing of cannons and muskets became very intense, and was described by Private Joshua H. Frier of the First Florida Infantry as a "sheet of flame."

Skirmishes continued throughout the morning of March 6, with the major fighting beginning around 11 a.m. Confederate forces, made up of about 600 men, fought off three major attacks and several minor attempts by Union forces of nearly equivalent strength. The Union troops, having decided that the bridge was impassable, began a hasty retreat. General Newton and his forces withdrew in mid-afternoon. Union soldiers felled trees to slow any pursuit. By the following morning, Newton's command was under the protection of the Navy fleet. Newton, feeling that the Navy had not adequately supported him, took his troops back to Key West. The Battle of Natural Bridge is considered quite an accomplishment by historians, the five day battle concluded when a motley militia of old men and young boys defeated seasoned Union troops. By this battle the interior of the state was again saved from invasion and its capital from seizure. Florida is the only Southern State east of the Mississippi River whose capital was not reached and occupied by the Union army. Natural Bridge was the last important Civil War battle in Florida. Union losses at the Battle of Natural Bridge totaled twenty-one killed, eighty-nine wounded, and 148 missing. Confederate losses were three killed and twenty-three wounded.

Ocklawaha Raiders

A wealthy planter, John Pearson became convinced early on that a War Between the States was inevitable and he bought muskets and other necessities for a company of 125 men he organized. Called the "Ocklawaha Raiders," the group, with Pearson as commander, was tendered to the governor even before the war began.

Battle of Olustee. On February 20, 1864 the largest Civil War battle on Florida soil occurred near Lake City and resulted in the defeat of the northern forces. This lithograph of the battle shows Black Union troops under intense fire from the 32nd and 64th Georgia regiments just before the Union advance was crushed.

Olustee Battle

Florida was not to be the scene of major battles during the Civil War because of its remote location. The Battle of Olustee (or Ocean Pond), February 20, 1864, was the major engagement of the Civil War in Florida. The campaign that culminated in the battle began when troops commanded by General Truman A. Seymour embarked at Hilton Head, South Carolina. Their immediate objective was a fourth occupation of Jacksonville. The force could then disrupt transportation links and deprive Confederate troops of food supplies from central Florida; capture cotton, turpentine and timber; gain black recruits for the Union army; and induce Unionists in east Florida to organize a loyal state government.

General Seymour's expeditionary force landed at Jacksonville on February 7. Scouts and raiders moved west and met little opposition. On February 9 they took Baldwin where they seized many supplies. By February 11 their cavalry had penetrated to within three miles of Lake City. At Lake City, Brigadier General Joseph Finegan was entrenched with a small force, and the Union army, supposing this force to be larger than it was, retreated to Sanderson.

Meanwhile, during the month of January, Confederate forces had noted movement of the Union fleet, and they began to prepare for an offensive. The defense of Florida was placed in the hands of General Finegan and Brigadier General Alfred Holt Colquitt. Once it was apparent the Union forces were moving westward in Florida, Finegan began searching for the Confederate army's best defendable position.

On February 13 General Finegan selected a position at Olustee. With a lake called Ocean Pond on his left, a nearly impassable swamp on his right and only a narrow passage between, he called for troops to help defend Florida. General Colquitt answered that call, bringing veteran troops from Savannah, Georgia.

Largest, Bloodiest Civil War Battle on Florida Soil. Confederate forces drove back the Union Army's attempt to march across north Florida and occupy Tallahassee, the capital of Florida. General Joseph Finegan was commander of the Confederate troops. General Truman Seymour was commander of the Union forces.

Olustee Battlefield Historic Memorial. The Olustee Battlefield State Historic Site covers 270 acres on U.S. Highway 90 two miles east of Olustee.

The Battle

Early on the morning of February 20, the Union force of 5,500 men and sixteen cannons marched westward from MacClenny. By this time, the Confederate forces almost equaled the Union opposing army in number. Finegan sent skirmishers to draw the Union forces to Olustee; they made contact that afternoon. The Confederate line was formed, and the infantry in the center was supported by cavalry on each flank.

The Union army approached in two columns: one by the railroad, the other by the Lake City and Jacksonville road. The battle was joined on the floor of a forest of virgin pines, free of underbrush. Men fought in the open forest; neither force constructed earthworks. The Union army used many black soldiers in this battle.

The battle lasted about six hours, and at the end the Union army gave way. General Finegan ordered a pursuit, which was continued until dark.

Results of the Battle

In this battle, the Confederates won a complete victory over the larger Union force. The State was saved from invasion, and valuable supplies of cotton, lumber, and provisions were preserved for the Confederacy. The Confederates captured several cannon and 1,600 stand of small arms. They also took a large number of prisoners.

Olustee was a bloody field. The Union loss was 203 killed, 1,152 wounded, 506 missing. Confederate

Olustee Battlefield. A museum offers exhibits that interpret this Confederate victory. The battlefield itself is well marked by a trail and signs along the battle lines.

Olustee Battle Reenactment. For two days each year the Civil War comes alive at the Olustee battleground site. For several days, the soldiers and civilian re-enactors "live" in the 1860s. They sleep on the ground, wear period clothing, eat hardtack, and listen to period music and church services so that life at the reenactment is as close as possible to the original. The battle reenactment involves the reenactors using horses and period equipment such a rifles and cannons.

Olustee Battle Reenactment.

losses were ninety-three killed, 847 wounded, and six missing.

Approximately 10,000 troops fought at Olustee, resulting in a total loss of almost 3,000 casualties (killed, wounded, and missing). None of the Union objectives had been met by entering Florida's interior.

In the haste of the Union retreat, General Seymour ordered 130,000 rounds of small arms ammunition dumped into the lake at Baldwin. The Confederates were able to salvage most of the balls or lead.

The Battle of Olustee was Florida's bloodiest Civil War battle and, for its size, one of the bloodiest battles of the entire war.

Palatka Battles

During the Civil War, Palatka was under fire of gunboats on the St. Johns River. At one time the city was occupied by 5,000 Union troops, supported by gunboats. The first Protestant Church in Palatka was St. Mark's Episcopal Church, built in 1852. The building was occupied during the Civil War, by Union troops.

The Bronson-Mulholland Place, a two-story house, was the home and estate of Judge Isaac H. Bronson. Because of its strategic position on the river it was occupied in turn by Union and Confederate soldiers during the Civil War.

Pensacola During the Civil War

For the most part, Pensacola was relatively quiet during the Civil War; however, there were occasional fireworks. On October 9, 1861, about 1,000 Confederate soldiers landed on Santa Rosa Island and attacked Union gun emplacements that had been erected outside Fort Pickens. The Confederates routed one encampment of Union troops but had to withdraw when Union soldiers from the fort joined the fight. This marked the first major battle of the Civil War in Florida. The casualties on both sides amounted to about 150 soldiers.

A few weeks later, Union troops reasserted their presence in Pensacola Bay by bombarding Confederate positions on the mainland. On November 22 and 23, the big guns of Fort Pickens, along with two Union gunboats, shelled Fort Barrancas, Fort McRee, and the Navy Yard. The Confederates returned the fire, and both sides suffered some damage.

On January 1, 1862 Union forces in Fort Pickens opened fire on Fort Barrancas and Confederate ships in the harbor. Confederates lobbed shells at Fort Pickens.

Confederate forces pulled out of Pensacola on May 9, 1862. A few days later, Pensacola and West Florida were back in Union hands. With the exception of some skirmishing around Fort Barrancas in August 1864, the

Pensacola Navy Yard Fireworks. A *Harper's Weekly* drawing of the Pensacola Navy Yard being heavily damaged during artillery duels of November 22 and 23, 1861.

Civil War had practically ended in Pensacola. In the latter years of the war, Fort Pickens was used as a prison for military and political prisoners.

Fort Pickens During the Civil War

Florida seceded from the Union in January 1861. By this time, Florida troops had captured and occupied Fort Marion (Castillo de San Marcos) in St. Augustine, the Union arsenal in Chattahoochee and Fort Clinch in Fernandina. Only two major coastal defenses remained — Fort Taylor at Key West and Fort Pickens in Pensacola — but the days of successful occupation of Union defenses had ended.

Learning that Florida soldiers had taken various Union fortifications and depots elsewhere in the state, Union soldiers stationed at Fort Barrancas spiked their guns and moved to Fort Pickens on January 10, 1861. Finding the fort in a rundown condition, the 80 plus Union force did what they could to put it into a defensive condition.

On April 12, 1861, Union troops landed on Santa Rosa Island to reinforce Fort Pickens. A few hours earlier, Confederate forces began bombarding Fort Sumter in South Carolina and the Civil War had begun.

In October 1861, Confederate soldiers attacked the Union encampment outside the walls of Fort Pickens and completely destroyed it. The guns of Fort Pickens were used in retaliation and as the months passed, events outside Florida ended any Confederate effort to hold coastal Florida.

On November 22 and 23, 1861, the guns of Fort Pickens joined those of two warships in driving the Confederates out of the other Pensacola forts. Fort Pickens helped make the Union blockade of the Gulf Coast effective throughout the rest of the war.

In May 1862, the Confederate force evacuated the Navy Yard and the town, and Union soldiers occupied Pensacola. Fort Pickens remained in Union hands throughout the Civil War; however, it saw very little action.

In the latter years of the war, Fort Pickens was used as a prison for military and political prisoners.

Fort Pickens was one of three forts that were never captured by the Confederates. Forts Taylor and Jefferson were also successfully kept from Confederate forces during the war.

Fort Pickens Battles. Located on Santa Rosa Island, near Pensacola, Fort Pickens was the scene of much active fighting during the first years of the Civil War.

Camp Sanderson

The site of Sanderson in Baker County was used by both Union and Confederate soldiers as a camp during the campaign of 1864. The camp was used as a Confederate supply depot, but it was abandoned on February 9, 1864. From the 9th to the 13th, it was held by Union troops and used as a base for raids on Lake City and Gainesville. On February 20 the site was used by Union troops attacking Olustee. In retreat from Olustee, the camp again fell into Confederate hands.

Santa Rosa Island Battle

On the night of October 9, 1861, General Anderson landed his Confederate troops on Santa Rosa Island surprising the New York 6th Volunteers at Billy Wilson's Zouaves Camp just east of Fort Pickens on Pensacola Bay. This marked the first major battle of the Civil War in Florida. The retreat of Union forces was halted by reinforcements from Fort Pickens, who drove the Confederates back to their boats in the early dawn. The casualties on both sides amounted to 154 men.

Seminoles During the Civil War

The Civil War caused further trouble and hardships for the Seminole Indians who had been forced to move to the Oklahoma Indian Territory. Pressure was put on their leaders from both the North and the South, and they were split into two groups.

One group, led by John Jumper, sided with the Confederates. The other group, led by Chief Billy Bowlegs and John Chupco, went over to the Union side. They had been urged to join the Confederates, but refused and moved north into Kansas territory. Both groups fought with distinction in the Civil War, on opposite sides. John Jumper became a Colonel in the Confederate Army.

Seville Skirmish

This small community is located at the northwest tip of Volusia County. A Civil War skirmish was fought on Braddock's farm.

Spring Garden Plantation

During the Civil War, the Thomas Stark family, owners of the Spring Garden Plantation, produced food to feed Confederate troops. The Sugar Mill was converted to grind corn. To stop such supplies from reaching their destination, Union forces from Jacksonville moved along the St. Johns River in April-May 1864. At Spring Garden, they seized cattle and cotton and demolished the buildings. The Union troops involved in the raid included several units of U.S. Colored Infantry.

St. Andrews Bay Skirmish

The U.S. Bark Roebuck, commanded by John Sherrill, was sent to St. Andrews Bay to prevent blockade running. On March 20, 1863, an eleven-man scouting party landed at a site near Panama City to secure fresh drinking water and was attacked by Confederates commanded by

A Surprise Attack on Santa Rosa Island.

Captain W. J. Robinson. When ordered to surrender, the Union crew refused and two were killed and six wounded in the ensuing skirmish. The rest escaped to their ship. The Confederates had no casualties.

St. Augustine During the Civil War

On March 12, 1862, Union forces arrived in St. Augustine to request the town's surrender. They were greeted by friendly politicians and local Unionists; the offer was quickly accepted and in short order the Stars and Stripes once again flew over Fort Marion. The occupying Union garrison found that there were many Southern sympathizers living in the city. These sympathizers were forced to leave.

The only real military opposition to the continued Union occupation was by a small Confederate cavalry force commanded by Captain John Dickison. Dickison occasionally raided the outskirts of St. Augustine, inflicting a few casualties and capturing some unlucky Union soldiers. In 1863, the Union Army made the town into a convalescent camp and hospital.

Slowly but steadily, the town's population grew with the arrival of more Union soldiers and with the growing number of disenchanted Confederate Army deserters.

In 1872, a tall stone obelisk was installed in the central plaza as mute testimony to the local men killed in the war. This monument still stands in the Plaza de la Constitution in downtown St. Augustine, guarded by 8-inch Rodman artillery pieces and a nearby 10-inch mortar, part of the wartime Fort Marion defenses.

Steamboat Battles During the Civil War

In 1862, Union forces captured the Confederate steamboat *Darlington*. With a crew of twenty-five Union troops and two 24-pound howitzers, the *Darlington* was put into Federal service. Later, the *Darlington* captured the Confederate steamboat *Governor Milton*.

On March 23, 1864, Union forces obtained information that a number of Confederate steamboats might be found on the headwaters of the St. Johns River or its tributaries. In early April, Master Champion and 1st Mate F. W. Sanborn, and twelve marines boarded the gunship *U.S.S. Columbine* at Palatka to undertake the perilous cruise. The next day Champion entered Lake George, and, after a short search found the *General Sumter*, a small sternwheel transport. With his prize, he returned to Palatka.

Several days later, a second expedition left Palatka with a Union crew aboard the *General Sumter*. As before, the *U S.S. Columbine* led the way. Champion moved up the river, and, upon reaching Lake Harney, Sanborn, aboard the *General Sumter*, found the *Hattie* hidden and disabled. The *Hattie* was repaired and put into service for the Union.

In May 1864, the *U.S.S. Columbine* was ambushed, and sunk, at Horse Landing, a few miles north of Lake George, by the Confederate troops of Captain John J. Dickison's 2nd Florida Cavalry using two light artillery pieces. This is the only incident in recorded U.S. history that cavalry destroyed a gunboat.

Union Picket Boat Shooting at Sharpshooters. Fernandina was a major supply terminal of the Confederacy. Shown is a Union phalanx river picket boat being attacked by Confederate sharpshooters stationed in the trees on the banks.

Saltworks Being Destroyed. During the Civil War, a Union officer sketched this destruction of a Confederate Salt Factory on St. Joseph's Bay by the crew of the *USS Kingfisher*. The drawing was published in *Harper's Weekly*, 1862.

Fort Steele

This temporary Civil War Confederate fort was established in 1861 in Mayport and named in honor of Dr. Holmes Steele.

St. Joseph Confederate Saltworks

A major Confederate saltworks, with a daily capacity of 150 bushels, was located in Port St. Joe. During the Civil War, salt processed by evaporation of seawater was one of Florida's chief contributions to the Confederacy. The saltworks were destroyed on September 8, 1862 by bombardment and landing party action from the *U.S.S. Kingfisher*.

St. Marks Lighthouse

Noted lighthouse builder, Winslow Lewis, began work on the St. Marks structure in 1829. Eroding shores forced relocation a short distance inland in 1842 to its present location in St. Marks. During the Civil War the lighthouse played a role in military affairs primarily because of its strategic position on the coast. Coastal raids launched from the blockading squadron comprised much of the hostile action against the Confederacy in Florida. One such raid in June of 1862 resulted in the destruction of a fortification located near the lighthouse. In response to the danger of raids of this nature, Confederate Army pickets were positioned in or near the lighthouse on a regular basis. To deter the use of the lighthouse as a lookout tower, a naval party landed and burned the steps and interior woodwork on July 15, 1863. In March of 1865 Union troops landed near the lighthouse for a major raid into the interior only to be repulsed at the Battle of Natural Bridge. Restored to service after the war, it resumed the role of a navigational aid for Gulf Coast commerce.

Tampa During the Civil War

The Civil War brought turbulent days to Tampa. The Confederates established extensive earthworks along the water side of the town. The trench was equipped with carts that were used as ammunition carriers. The waterfront was further protected with the emplacement of five guns. These defenses, however, were never used because whenever the Union forces landed they flanked the town from a different direction. Tampa was bombarded three times by Union gunboats; however, little damage was done to the village. In 1862, several Confederate Army soldiers were captured by the Union forces and imprisoned at Fort Marion, for the duration of the conflict.

During the war Tampa had become almost a ghost town. The local government was suspended and the town fell into ruin. In 1866, after the Civil War clouds had cleared, many former residents of Tampa returned and started rebuilding the town.

Postcard View of Fort Taylor.

Fort Zachary Taylor

Construction of the fort named for General Zachary Taylor, the twelfth President of the United States, began in 1845. General Taylor was in command of the United States troops during the early part of the Second Seminole War. This fort is one of a series of forts built to defend the coastlines of the United States. The building of these forts was a result of the War of 1812 when the British were able to invade the United States on three fronts without a significant challenge. When finished, Fort Taylor was strategically one of the most important forts in the United States because it defended not only the waters around Key West, but also controlled the surrounding waterways of the Straits of Florida and Gulf of Mexico.

Yet, due primarily to the lack of construction materials, it took over twenty years to complete Fort Taylor. Other reasons for the long construction time are attributed to hurricanes and disease. By 1860 the fort was ready to hold troops and cannon.

By the time the three-story fort was finally finished in 1866, there were many impressive features included. Items such as sanitary facilities flushed by the tide and a desalination plant that produced drinking water from the sea were available as early as 1861. The main structure is in the form of a trapezoid-quadrilateral, with two sides parallel, built 1,000 feet offshore on an underwater foundation of granite blocks shipped from New England. Each of the three seaward walls extends 255 feet and the landward wall is 495 feet. A total of 198 guns and a large supply of ammunition were on hand to secure the fort.

Through an arched door, Sally Port, a long causeway, connected the fort to Key West. Stairways on each side of the Sally Port led to the second and third levels, the sleeping quarters for the troops.

During the Civil War

When the Civil War broke out in 1861, Captain John Brannon and his company of forty-four men occupied the fort, placing it in Union hands. Key West was an important outpost for the Union because numerous

Fort Taylor During the Civil War. Fort Taylor's role during the Civil War was to serve as a base of operations for the Union Navy to prevent supply ships from reaching Confederate ports.

Rodman Cannon at Fort Taylor. Fort Taylor's 198 guns were located in two floors of gunrooms, and along the top of each fort wall. Shown is a cannon on the north wall, facing the approach to Key West harbor.

Courtyard of Fort Zachary Taylor. Fort Taylor remained in Union hands throughout the Civil War. Soldiers died at the fort during the war, but they were felled by yellow fever, not Confederate troops.

blockade-running ships were detained at Key West harbor and guarded by Fort Taylor's cannons. The 10-inch Rodman and Columbiad cannons at the fort had a range of three miles. This was an impressive deterrent to the Confederate Navy, preventing them from attempting to take the fort or the island of Key West. The fort's role during the Civil War was to serve as a base of operations for the Union Navy's Gulf Coast Blockade Squadron. That group prevented supply ships from reaching Confederate ports.

Fort Taylor's five-foot thick walls rose fifty feet above the water, and the three-mile range of the fort's cannons at one point held 299 Confederate ships in Key West harbor. Shaped like a trapezoid, the structure originally was located a quarter mile offshore but silt and dredge fill over the years have caused the fort to become landlocked. Proving to be a severe loss for the South, Fort Taylor remained in Union hands throughout the Civil War. Union soldiers died at Fort Taylor during the Civil War, but they were felled by yellow fever, not Confederate troops.

Union Prisoners of War

During the Civil War, approximately 194,000 Union Prisoners of War (POW) were sent to Southern prisons.

U.S.S. Fort Henry

A Union gunboat, the *U.S.S. Fort Henry* patrolled fifty miles of Florida's northwest coastline and occasionally confronted Confederate blockade-runners. Lieutenant Commander Edward Yorke McCauley commanded this 150-foot sidewheel steam powered boat, armed with six large guns. The crew of the *U.S.S. Fort Henry* also used small launches to engage Confederate infantry along Florida's Gulf Coast shoreline. Numerous Confederate ships were captured or destroyed by the men of the *U.S.S. Fort Henry* including the schooner *Anna Maria* and sloops *G. L. Brockenborough*, *Emma*, and *Isabella*.

Fort Walton

Fort Walton Beach in the Florida Panhandle now occupies the site of the former Fort Walton. The fort was named for Colonel George Walton, who was secretary of West Florida during Andrew Jackson's governorship, and the son of George Walton, a signer of the Declaration of Independence. During the Civil War, a Confederate installation, originally called Camp Walton, was constructed in 1861 to guard East Pass and garrisoned by a company of Florida militia called the "Walton Guards." Several small skirmishes with federal landing parties occurred near here. The Camp was abandoned following the Confederate evacuation of Pensacola, and the garrison, a part of the First Florida Infantry Regiment, was assigned to duty on the Tennessee front in early 1862.

Fort Ward

When Florida seceded from the U.S. in 1861, the state's seaports became vulnerable to attacks from the Union Navy. To protect shipping at St. Marks, Confederate forces built Fort Ward on the site of an old Spanish fort. The north wall was built with loose debris and earth, and was braced with rows of wooden posts. The embankment was high enough to hide the soldiers while standing up. Behind the wall, the garrison filled and leveled the old Spanish moat to serve as the fort's main floor. Cannons were mounted to dominate both the St. Marks and Wakulla rivers

Fort Ward remained active from the time Confederate forces moved in to occupy it in 1861 until the first surrender May 12, 1865. Although no famous battle took place, the fort's presence discouraged the blockading Union naval forces from driving inland from the Gulf of Mexico.

Earthen and wooden barricades were built over the foundations of the old Spanish fort, San Marcos De Apalache, which was formerly located here. Union naval officers, who had established an effective blockade off the mouth of the St. Marys River, regarded the Confederate batteries of St. Marks with great respect. Fort Ward kept St. Marks and the upriver town of Newport secure until the Union invasion of 1865.

Welaka

Union troops occupied an outpost near Welaka in an attempt to stop the flow of food and supplies meant for Confederate troops along the St. Johns River.

Yellow Bluff Fort

The Confederate Yellow Bluff Fort was built in 1862 to prevent Union gunboats from attacking Jacksonville. Cannons positioned at the fort could fire on approaching boats on the St. Johns River from behind a protective cover of trees.

Located on the north side of the St. Johns River, on the New Berlin Road in Jacksonville, Yellow Bluff Fort was one of two major Confederate fortifications on the river (the other being St. Johns Bluff) to control the passage of enemy gunboats up the river to Jacksonville. The placement of an earthwork fort on the 90-foot-high bluff was originally suggested or designed by General Robert E. Lee in 1861 while surveying coast defenses. Later, in 1862, he recommended to Brigadier General J. H. Trapier that the proposed Yellow Bluff fortification be used as the main defense before Jacksonville. Before this could be fully enforced, Union forces attacked and reduced the fortifications on St. Johns Bluff, causing the evacuation of Yellow Bluff by the Confederates. It was later reoccupied by Confederate forces under Captain John J. Dickison, refortified, and withstood repeated attacks by Union gunboats. In 1864, Union forces again occupied Yellow Bluff when the Confederates evacuated the works, and established a signal station there, used until the end of the war.

Yulee Sugar Mill Raid

The Yulee Sugar Mill and Plantation, in Homosassa, on the Gulf Coast, was a vital source of food supplies for the Confederate Army. The Mill and Plantation was raided by Union troops at the height of the war and burned to the ground. The remains of the old stone mill are intact and the site is designated as a Historical Monument, maintained by the Florida State Forestry Service. An annual Civil War reenactment, named the Yulee Sugar Mill Battle, is held in nearby Crystal River. Here the generals in gray and blue muster their troops and scores of infantrymen, artillery units, and dashing cavalry riders fight much as their ancestors did in the 1860s.

5

World War I and II Military Bases

World War I and II were terrible experiences shared by Americans from all walks of life, race, gender, and economical backgrounds. All worked and sacrificed together in a common cause to defeat the powerful forces of militarism that sought to dominate the entire world.

Floridians united against the forces of evil by turning the state into an industrial arsenal for war material and a vast network of military bases to be used for the training of American and Allied troops.

Army Machine Gunner in World War I.

World War I

On April 6, 1917 the United States became involved in World War I and declared war on Germany. Over 42,000 Floridians served in the armed services during this war. Almost 1,300 Floridians were killed in action.

During World War I, Florida became the training grounds for the military. Major military and training centers were established throughout the state. World War I ended in 1918.

Chow Call—
A U.S. Army Kitchen during World War I.

World War II

On Pearl Harbor Day, December 7, 1941, when Floridians learned that the United States had been thrown into the world conflict that had been raging in Europe for over two years, most of the state's population lived in rural, agricultural regions with little industry of any consequence. Because Japan was an ally of Germany, the United States declared war on both nations.

The war brought dramatic changes to the state. Florida's strategic location made the state vital for national defense, and dozens of military installations were activated before and during the war. A tremendous migration of military personnel into the area took place. Florida, once again, became the grounds for military training. A new naval air station was established at Jacksonville. An Army training center was established at Camp Blanding, near Starke. Pensacola's naval base was the scene of increased activity. Naval bases were reactivated at Key West. Many flying schools and pilot training bases were established throughout the state. By 1945, Florida had forty airfields in operation. Eglin Field, near Pensacola; Drew and McDill Fields in Tampa; Dale Mabry Field in Tallahassee; Buckingham and Page Airfields in Fort Myers; Panama City's Tyndall Army Airfield; and Avon Park, Boca Raton, Homestead, Sarasota, and Venice Army Airfields were very active air bases throughout WWII. Camp Gordon Johnston at Carrabelle became an active amphibious warfare-training center. By 1943 there were 172 military installations in existence in Florida.

Banana River Naval Air Station. In 1940 the Banana River Naval Air Station opened on a narrow strip of barrier island roughly located between Melbourne and Cocoa Beach. During World War II this station supported coastal seaplane patrol operations and operated a PBM seaplane pilot training program and advanced navigation school. In 1949 the military base became the Patrick Air Force Base.

Naval bases and air stations were established or expanded at Daytona Beach, DeLand, Fort Lauderdale, Green Cove Springs, Jacksonville, Melbourne, Miami, Richmond, Sanford and Vero Beach. In Fort Pierce, some 150,000 Army, Marine Corps, and Navy personnel passed through amphibious training. The Coast Guard established a training center in St. Augustine.

Many of Florida's tourist facilities were converted to wartime needs. Throughout the state every major resort city turned its principal hotels over to some branch of armed services. Resort hotels were used as training centers, convalescent homes, barracks and hospitals. Florida's colleges and universities were used as training sites as well as living quarters for military personnel.

Civilian spotters were used along Florida's coast to protect the state from aircraft or German U-boat attacks. By 1943, more than 300,000 had volunteered for civilian defense activities.

"Peace Comes to World" announced the *Jacksonville Florida Times Union* newspaper on V-J Day, August 15, 1945. World War II formally ended on September 2, 1945. More than a quarter-million Floridians—a fifth of the population—served in World War II and its immediate aftermath. Thousands of Florida's sons and daughters had served in combat theaters around the world. More than 4,600 Floridians serving in the armed forces died during the war, with battle deaths numbering 3,174.

World War II in Fort Pierce. Protective barrier islands along the Florida Atlantic Coast made Fort Pierce an ideal location for training in amphibious warfare. The U.S. Navy established an Amphibious Training Base here in early 1943. Servicemen were trained as small and large landing craft crews, combat engineers, salvage crews and construction personnel (Seabees). More than 110,000 personnel were trained here before the base was decommissioned in 1946.

Camp Blanding

Planned in 1939 to train the National Guard of Florida and other Southern states, the post's construction began in December 1940 and was taken over by the U.S. War Department. The camp was a major Army training post during WWII, and is now a state-operated post for the training of the Florida National Guard, U.S. Army reservists, and regular U.S. Army units. The camp is located ten miles east of Starke and twenty miles southwest of Jacksonville. The 180,000-acre reservation on Lake Kingsley was named for Lieutenant General Albert H. Blanding.

At peak times during World War II, Camp Blanding personnel were training up to 80,000 soldiers. Between 1940 and 1945 more than 800,000 recruits were trained at Camp Blanding. Famous World War II U.S. Army divisions trained at Camp Blanding were the 1st, 29th, 30th, 31st, 36th, 43rd, 63rd, 66th and 79th Infantry Divisions. In WWII the 508th Parachute Infantry Regiment (PIR) was formed and trained here, and many individual soldiers of the Infantry Replacement Training Center (IRTC) supplied replacements to Army units throughout the world. Separate Field Artillery, Cavalry, Engineer and Infantry regiments prepared for WWII in sand pine and scrub oak areas on this desolate piece of Florida wilderness.

In 1942, while being known as Florida's fourth largest city, Camp Blanding became home to detained

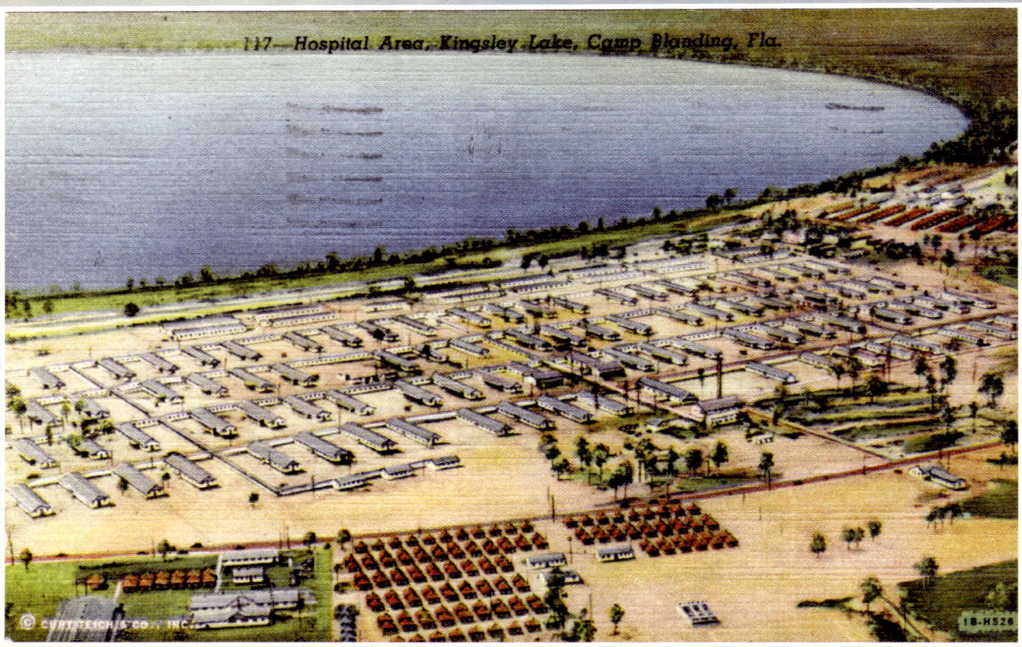

Camp Blanding Hospital and Reception Center. The Camp Blanding Hospital, located northeast of Kingsley Lake, consisted of over 200 buildings, with connecting covered walkways. This hospital accommodated more than 2,000 patients. The groups of tents shown in lower center foreground formed the reception center where all volunteers and selectees from this area were inducted and assigned to their place of training.

Camp Blanding. Florida's fourth largest city during World War II, the complex, conceived in 1939 as a summer camp for the Florida National Guard, grew to 180,000 acres and provided housing to 55,000 Army personnel. Camp Blanding is located near Starke and Jacksonville.

Company Street at Camp Blanding.
In 1942, soldiers lived in barracks and tents overlooking Lake Kingsley.

Soldiers on Leave in Starke.
Soldiers at Camp Blanding spent their time off visiting the nearest city — Starke. A soldier from Texas sent the above postcard home to his mother and said, "This is really a soldier's town."

Parade Ground.
Passing in review was a common sight at Camp Blanding.

German citizens and prisoners. During World War II, Camp Blanding became the largest POW (Prisoner of War) camp in Florida with upwards of 1,000 prisoners at any time.

Preserving the Past

The Camp Blanding Museum is located in one of the camp's WWII barracks. Visitors to the museum will find many artifacts, exhibits, photographs, and documents of the period. Numerous World War II-era military vehicles are also located on the grounds, including an M4 Sherman Tank, M3 Half Track, M16 Half Track, an original C-47 paratrooper plane, jeeps, armored trucks, airplanes, helicopters, cannons, and many other vintage military vehicles and guns. You can also walk the trenches of a full-sized replica U.S. "Firebase" fortification as used in Vietnam, and also see original "Russian" IRAQI tanks from Operation Desert Storm. The Museum and Memorial Park is located inside the Main Gate at Camp Blanding.

Service Company at Camp Blanding. An estimated 800,000 soldiers were trained during World War II. It was also the largest POW camp in Florida with upwards of 1,000 German prisoners at any time.

Soldiers Attending the Ritz Theater. The Ritz Theater in Starke was a popular recreational destination for Camp Blanding soldiers on leave.

Camp Blanding Museum.

Florida Regimental Memorial at the Museum. This memorial was dedicated November 25, 1990, to the memory of the men of the Florida National Guard, who sacrificed their lives during World War II. Members of the Guard served in the Pacific and European Theaters of Operation.

M4 Sherman Tank. Several World War II tanks are on display at Camp Blanding Museum.

Douglas C-47A Transport at the Museum. During World War II, no aircraft of the U.S. Army Air Force was more widely known and saw more service than the "Gooney Bird." Produced in greater numbers than any other transport, the C-47 served in every combat area of the war as a troop transport, freight plane, and tow plane for troop carriers. Over 10,000 C-47s of all types were built, including the DC-3, the commercial version, which was used for many years after the war. Olive drab on top, pale gray underneath. National insignia — white star, blue circle, white bars outlined in dark blue, with red stripes in center of bars — on fuselage.

German 105mm Howitzer. A German, Russian, and several American WWII Howitzer guns are displayed at Camp Blanding Museum.

Buckingham Army Airfield

Located in a rural area near Fort Myers, this airfield was established in 1942 as a gunnery school, with 50,000 aircrew gunners were trained on B-17 Flying Fortress and B-24 Liberator bombers. After World War II the base was returned to the City of Fort Myers.

Carlstrom Field

Located in Arcadia and named for World War I pilot Lieutenant Victor Carlstrom, the field served as the U.S. Army's principal flying school until 1923. In 1941, Royal Air Force aviators were trained there.

Fort Clinch

This fort was pressed into service by the U.S. Armed Forces one last time during World War II. The Coast Guard, in a joint operation with the Army and the Navy, established and maintained a surveillance and communications system within the fort and on various coastal islands in the area. This operation included the Coast Guard's mounted beach patrol, which kept watch along the beaches for landings by spies and saboteurs.

Coastal Defense Towers

Following the Japanese attack on Pearl Harbor December 7, 1941, the American government placed a high priority on Civil Defense throughout World War II. There were 489 observation towers established along Florida coasts by October 1942. Plans called for the eventual establishment of 850 such towers throughout the state. The purpose was to provide a virtual 'picket fence" of civilian observers to warn of an impending attack. Local citizens, trained to recognize aircraft and submarines, became volunteer members of the Ground Observation Corps. Working in two-person shifts, observers maintained 24-hour coverage. The observation towers were abandoned in May of 1944 when it became apparent the Germans no longer posed a threat to our coastline. Few towers survived after the war.

Corry Field

Established by the U.S. Navy at Pensacola in 1928, the base was named to honor Quincy native and Medal of Honor recipient Lieutenant Commander William M. Corry, Jr., who was killed while attempting to save a fellow aviator from a burning airplane. During World War II, Corry Field became an important training center for American and British pilots. In addition, naval aviators received training in dive-bombing and torpedo bombing at this base. With six outlying airfields in 1944, the site complement consisted of over 2,500 military personnel.

Dale Mabry Field

Established as a U.S. Army base in January 1941, it was named in honor of Army Captain Dale Mabry, who died in an airship crash in 1922. The airfield, located in Tallahassee, occupied over 1,700 acres and over 130 buildings during the course of World War II. Army pilots were trained on P-39 Airacobra, P-40 Warhawk, and P-47 Thunderbolt aircraft. Chinese and French cadets received training here in 1942 and 1944. In mid-1944 the

World War II Defense Tower. This defense tower, located at Ormond-by-the-Sea, is thought to be the only remaining such structure on the Florida Atlantic coast. The tower was constructed and staffed by civilian volunteer "spotters," armed only with binoculars and a telephone, who monitored the skies and coastline for enemy airplanes and German U-boats.

Corry Field. Prior to World War II, Corry Field, in Pensacola, served as a primary training field. During World War II the Navy flew anti-submarine patrols and air-sea rescue planes from Corry.

WAAC Training in Daytona Beach. An important part of Basic Training at the WAAC Center was the physical exercises conducted on the beach. The "fatigue" dresses were pale green and white stripe seersucker. Hats and socks were khaki color.

air base complement averaged over 5,000 military and civilian personnel. Today, the air base site is the home of Tallahassee Community College.

Daytona Beach

In December 1942 the U.S. Navy established flight training at the Daytona Beach Municipal Airport. Nearly 1,500 officers and enlisted men were stationed at NAS Daytona Beach. Flight training was first provided here on SBD Dauntless Dive Bombers and SNC-1 Falcons, and later F4F Wildcat, FM-1, and F6F Hellcat aircraft. Four outlying airfields were employed at Bunnell, New Smyrna Beach, Ormond Beach, and Spruce Creek. The New Smyrna Beach airfield included a launch catapult and arresting gear equipped to accommodate basic aircraft carrier training. At the end of World War II, the Daytona Beach airfield reverted back to local officials and became the present day Daytona Beach International Airport.

In addition to the Naval Air Station, the WAAC Training Center and Welch Convalescent Center were also located in Daytona Beach. At the peak of the Welch Center's operation, it housed about 6,000 patients, enlisted personnel and officers, and employed nearly 800 residents.

DeLand Naval Air Station

During World War II, thousands of aviators were trained at the Naval Air Station in DeLand. They learned targeting, tactics, and teamwork on Douglas Dauntless SBD Dive Bombers, Flying Venturas, and F6F Hellcat carrier-based fighters. More than a hundred structures were on the base: ammo bunkers, fuel tanks, heating plant, hospital, firehouse, hangers, classrooms, barracks, brig, refrigeration plant, and other facilities. Nearly all the military structures are gone, replaced by modern businesses and warehouses.

Over 330 officers and 1,100 enlisted personnel were stationed at this site by early 1944. NAS DeLand maintained an outlying field at the Spruce Creek Airport in Port Orange for carrier landing training.

DeLand Naval Air Station. The Naval Training Command trained combat dive-bomber pilots flying the Douglas Dauntless SBD in DeLand from 1942 to 1946. The plane was critical to the success of World War II battles in the Pacific. Today a museum is located here.

Dinner Key Naval Air Facility

The nation's first Naval Air Station was established at Dinner Key, south of Miami, in 1917. This site originally saw duty as a seaplane and dirigible base. NAF Dinner Key was established in 1943. During World War II, the base was used by the Navy for training and by the Coast Guard for flight operations. Personnel at the base averaged over 700 during the war. NAF Dinner Key was decommissioned after the war ended.

Doolittle Raid

On April 18, 1942, sixteen American Mitchell B-25 bombers led by Lieutenant Colonel James H. Doolittle took off from the *Hornet* aircraft carrier to bomb Japan. It was one of the first offensive actions of World War II and raised American morale at a time when it was desperately needed.

Doolittle and his men trained at one of Eglin Field's auxiliary airfields while their B-25 bombers were being modified. By the end of their training, the pilots were able to take off using only 350 feet of runway. After Doolittle and his men attacked Tokyo and a number of other Japanese cities, they bailed out or crashed in China.

Drane Field

Lakeland Army Airfield was originally constructed for the City of Lakeland in mid-1942 and named Drane Field to honor congressman Herbert Jackson Drane. The training school produced pilots for B-17 and B-24 bombers. Pilots from England, Greece, and other countries were also trained here.

Drew Army Airfield

Drew Field Municipal Airport opened in 1928 on land previously owned by developer John H. Drew. During World War II, with the completion of nearby MacDill Army Airfield, Drew became headquarters for the III Fighter Command. Encompassing fifteen square miles and hosting a complement of up to 25,000 personnel, Drew Army Airfield provided training for heavy bomber crews. During the war, 1,000 combat bombing crews trained at Drew. After the war ended the airfield became Tampa International Airport.

Drew Field.
Drew Field, located in Tampa, was an important airfield during World War II, providing training for heavy bomber crews. In 1939, the city of Tampa leased Drew Field to the Army, which turned it into a military facility with improved runways.

Dunnellon Army Airfield

Opened in 1942 to train pilots and crewmen for the British-designed Horsa glider and C-47 Skytrain, after World War II ended, the site was returned for use as a municipal airport.

Eglin Air Force Base

Located near Valparaiso and Fort Walton Beach, this is one of the largest Air Force bases in the world. It consists of 724 square miles of land ranges and almost 98,000 square miles of water ranges. In 1941, Eglin became a training site for Army Air Force fighter pilots. Jimmy Doolittle, a famous World War II pilot, trained his B-25 strike force for their raid against Tokyo at Eglin Air Force Base.

Originally established on June 14, 1935, as Valparaiso Bombing and Gunnery Range with 1,460 acres of land donated by James E. Plew, this site was renamed on August 4, 1937, for Lieutenant Colonel Frederick I. Eglin, killed in an airplane crash. Eglin Field became a separate operating base August 27, 1940.

By the end of World War II, Eglin was the second largest air facility in the U.S. As with many other facilities during the war, Eglin hosted up to 300 German prisoners of war. Following the surrender of Germany in May 1945, German V-2 rockets were evaluated at this facility.

Eglin-Hurlburt Field Airdrome

Eglin-Hurlburt Field Airdrome, an Eglin Air Force Auxiliary Field, was named in honor of Lieutenant Donald Wilson Hurlburt, a distinguished World War II combat pilot. It is located six miles west of Eglin Air Force Base. Special operations, electronics, and radar countermeasure training took place at this facility during World War II.

Embry-Riddle Aeronautical University

Called by some the "Harvard of the Sky," the four-year university next to Daytona Beach Regional Airport has become known worldwide for turning out highly qualified personnel skilled in aeronautical engineering, aviation management, and aircraft engineering technology. The university started in 1926 as a small pilot training school. On December 7, 1941, Embry-Riddle had eighty-seven flight instructors ready to train aviators.

During WWII, the Embry-Riddle School of Aviation trained more than 2,000 British Royal Air Force (RAF) fliers and about one-tenth of all American pilots, along with thousands of mechanics and aviation workers. By the war's end, the school had trained more than 26,000 men and women in all fields of aviation, thus providing invaluable assistance to the Allied effort.

In 1961, the school became a nonprofit educational institution and today has 5,000 students; it's the second largest private university in Florida and is the only fully accredited aviation-oriented university in the world. The school's extended campus enrollment is more than 15,000 students located on over 100 extended campuses in the U.S. and several European countries.

Florida National Guard in World War II

World War II was one of the most significant and largest wars in all history. The men of Florida's Army National Guard served, trained, fought, and died in every theater of operations and every great land and air battle of that titanic global struggle; many served in or with the infantry. Most came home at war's end; some did not. Although nearly all of Florida's Guardsmen were mobilized in 1940 as part of the 31st Infantry Division, most saw service with other units. The Guardsmen were trained at Camp Blanding in northeast Florida.

For those Florida Guardsmen who went into combat with the 31st Infantry Division, the war was fought in the jungles of New Guinea and the enemy-held islands off its northwestern coast. They then participated in the long and costly campaign to free the island of Mindanao in the southern Philippines from Japanese control. Scheduled for the invasion of Japan itself, Florida's Guardsmen in the 31st Division were spared that potentially costly experience by the war-ending impact of the atomic bombs dropped on Hiroshima and Nagasaki.

Of the approximately 4,000 Florida Guardsmen mobilized in federal service during 1940 and 1941, two hundred are known to have died, killed in action, or died of wounds during the war. Many hundreds more were wounded, but survived to return home at war's end.

Camp J. Clifford R. Foster

In World War I troops were trained at Camp Joseph E. Johnston on Black Point about twelve miles from Jacksonville, established in 1909 as a Florida National Guard camp. Site of the second largest rifle range in the U.S., it was renamed Camp J. Clifford R. Foster after World War I and again occupied by the National Guard. During World War II the site was converted into the Jacksonville Naval Air Station.

Main Gate at Camp J. Clifford R. Foster.

German Submarines

During World War II German U-boats sank nearly 400 U.S. ships, including nearly fifty off Florida's coast. On April 10, 1942 the German U-123 submarine torpedoed the tanker Gulfamerica off Jacksonville Beach. The resulting fiery explosion was clearly seen onshore and curious crowds gathered to view the ships destruction. On July 18, 1943 the German U-134 submarine shot down the U.S. Navy blimp K-74 in the Florida Keys.

Eventually, Navy combat ships were employed in convoy duty, antisubmarine craft were built, and spotting stations were established along the Florida coast. Once these defensive measures were implemented, losses from German U-boat attacks along Florida coasts declined dramatically throughout the remainder of World War II.

Although U.S. forces off Florida attacked several German U-boats, only two were confirmed sunk. In one action, the U.S. Coast Guard vessel *Thetis* dropped depth charges to sink the German submarine U-157 southwest of Key West.

German U-Boat Landing

On the night of June 16, 1942, German submarine U-584 landed four trained Nazi agents on the Atlantic Coast in present day Ponte Vedra Beach dressed as American civilians. After burying four boxes containing explosives and incendiaries in the sand, they boarded a bus en route to New York to rendezvous with another team of saboteurs. Two members of the New York team betrayed the operation to the FBI. All were apprehended, tried and convicted. The informers went to prison and the others were electrocuted on August 8, 1942.

Tankers and Freighters Attacked By German U-Boats. Twenty-four U.S. and Allied freighters and tankers were sunk in Florida coastal waters by German submarines (U-boats) during World War II. Many torpedoed merchant vessels could be see burning from the beach and balconies of tourist hotels along the Atlantic coast. Shown is a stricken tanker burning off Hope Sound.

U.S. Subchaser Looking for German Subs.

Mothball Fleet in Green Cove Springs. Shown here is a small section of U.S. Navy ships moored at the Green Cover Springs Naval Station. The ships were put in a state of preservation just after World War II, to await their country's call to duty.

Green Cove Springs

Between 1940 and 1945, the population of Green Cove Springs increased from 1,752 to 3,026 as a result of the wartime construction of Benjamin Lee Field, a 1,500-acre air auxiliary complex, by the U.S. Navy. Aircraft checkout and carrier qualifications using F4F Wildcats and F4U Corsairs were performed at the complex. The station complement numbered over 2,000 Navy personnel in 1944. With the end of World War II, thirteen piers were constructed by the Navy and the Green Cove base became homeport to a "mothball fleet" of some 600 ships.

Hendricks Army Airfield

Established in January 1942 as a B-17 Flying Fortress training facility, the airfield, located in Sebring, had a complement of 2,600 military personnel. At the height of operations, as many as 7,000 weekly takeoffs and landings were common. During the early stages of World War II, B-17 bombers flew from Hendricks Airfield on submarine patrol along the Atlantic Coast. The facility, deactivated in 1945, is now Sebring Municipal Airport. A refurbished World War II-era control tower and other artifacts are located at the airport.

U.S. Naval Air Station.
In 1940 the former site of Camp Joseph E. Johnston and Camp J. Clifford R. Foster was converted into the Naval Air Station Jacksonville. NAS Jacksonville became one of the three largest naval air stations in the world. The U.S. Naval Air Station was commissioned in 1940, and housed over 42,000 Navy personnel and 11,000 civilians at its height during wartime activity.

HMS Mica

This British Liberty ship was torpedoed in 1942 by a German U-Boat in the Gulf of Mexico twenty-five miles south of Apalachicola. The fourteen survivors were cared for in the Apalachicola Armory.

Homestead Army Airfield

Established in 1942 on the site of South Dade County Airport in Homestead, this World War II post was a departure point for shipment of transport aircraft via South America and Africa to the Middle East and the China-Burma-Indian Theater. By 1943 the airfield specialized in training transport pilots and crews.

Jacksonville Naval Air Station

The Naval Air Station at Black Point in Jacksonville was established in October 1940, on the former site of Camp J. Clifford R. Foster. NAS Jacksonville became one of the three largest Naval Air Stations in the world. Pilot training began in 1941. During 1943 and 1944 with a peak of 1,000 aircraft, two takeoffs and landings occurred each minute, on a 24-hour basis. By 1945 NAS Jacksonville housed over 42,000 Navy personnel and 11,000 civilian employees. The auxiliary naval airfields at Cecil Field (Jacksonville), Green Cove Springs and Mayport (Jacksonville) served the aviators from this station. After World War II ended in 1945, NAS Jacksonville became a large separation center. Camp Blanding transferred German POWs (Prisoners Of War) to the base in 1945.

Plane being catapulted at the Naval Air Station, Jacksonville.

Naval Hospital.
The hospital is one of the major commands located at the Jacksonville Naval Air Station.

Jacksonville NAS Administration Building.

U. S. Navy Bombers Over Jacksonville Beach.

CAMP GORDON JOHNSTON

In June 1942 the U.S. War department selected a 165,000-acre section of coastal Franklin County to be used as an amphibious warfare training center. Originally called Camp Carrabelle, the base was renamed in January 1943 to honor the memory of Colonel Gordon Johnston, who had died in 1934. Colonel Johnston had served in the early twentieth century, won a Medal of Honor for his actions in the Philippines, and later fought in France during World War I.

The 3rd Engineer Amphibian Brigade arrived for training on September 10, 1942. The second largest army facility in Florida during World War II, the base was known by troops stationed there as "Hell-by-the-Sea" because of its crude living conditions and dangerous training programs. The Army deliberately made Camp Gordon Johnston primitive and dangerous to simulate the hardships of fighting and to prepare the men for the horrors and brutalities they would be facing on the battlefronts, especially D-Day in June 1944.

The 4th, 28th and 38th Infantry Divisions also received training at the base. Its mission was changed in September 1943 to train personnel to operate small harbor craft and amphibious vehicles. In late 1943 Carrabelle Beach and Dog Island, while they were a part of Camp Gordon Johnston, were used by the U.S. Army 4th Infantry Division to train for the Normandy Invasion on D-Day, June 6th, 1944. During this period, the base was home to more than 30,000 troops.

Amphibious Truck at Camp Johnston. In 1943 Camp Gordon Johnston at Carrabelle was used as a location for training men in the operation of the DUKW Amphibious Truck, a vehicle that revolutionized amphibian warfare.

General Omar Bradley, who would become the leader of the American Ground Forces in France during WWII, trained in Camp Gordon Johnston. Airborne exercises were conducted in the area by paratroopers from Fort Benning, Georgia. In 1944, German and Italian prisoners of war were interned at the camp. The end of World War II in August 1945 made Camp Gordon Johnston obsolete, and it was decommissioned in 1946. Around a quarter of a million soldiers trained at Camp Gordon Johnston.

Camp Joseph E. Johnston

Created on October 13, 1916 at Black Point, about twelve miles from Jacksonville on a former Florida National Guard camp; the post was named after Confederate General Joseph E. Johnston, who had been quartermaster general of the U.S. Army in 1860 and was the site of the second largest rifle range in the United States. With the arrival of the first 27,000 military personnel, orders for goods and services had a growing impact on Jacksonville's economy. Jacksonville was full of soldiers who received training at Camp Joseph E. Johnston. America's involvement in World War I lasted only nineteen months, but it shook Jacksonville just as it jarred the nation. The cantonment of 825 buildings on the 3,036-acre reservation was closed on June 28, 1919, after which time the site was renamed Camp Foster and again occupied by the National Guard. During World War II the site was converted into the Jacksonville Naval Air Station.

Kay Larkin Field

Established in 1943 in Palatka and named for Putnam County's first war casualty, Jaspar Kennedy "Kay" Larkin, the U.S. Navy post was designated as an auxiliary field to the Jacksonville Naval Air Station. Gunnery flights were also conducted between this airfield and the Naval Air Station in Green Cove Springs. After World War II, the site resumed use as a civilian airfield.

Key West Naval Air Station

Originated in 1823 as a base from which American naval forces could suppress pirates in the Caribbean and Gulf of Mexico, in 1940 the base was designated NAS Key West. Using four destroyers and three submarines, the Navy operated a sonar sound school at this station. PBM Mariner and OSZU Kingfisher aircraft operated here. During World War II, with the German U-boat threat to Atlantic Ocean shipping, Key West became an assembly

Camp Joseph E. Johnston. In 1909, a Florida National Guard camp was established on Black Point. During World War I (1917-1918) the camp was converted to Camp Joseph E. Johnston to train quartermaster troops.

Troops at Camp Johnston. During WWI (1917-1918) over 27,000 military personnel were trained at Camp Joseph E. Johnston. It was renamed Camp J. Clifford R. Foster after the war and again occupied by the National Guard. Black Point was converted into one of the largest military air installations in this country during WWII (1941-1945).

NAS Key West.

Main Gate to Key West NAS. PBM Mariner, OSZU Kingfisher aircraft and U.S. Navy blimps operated here during World War II. The blimps carried electronic equipment for aircraft early-warning and anti-submarine missions during the war.

point for convoys. Meacham Field, the Key West Municipal Airport, became an outlying field for NAS Key West and a base for a blimp utility squadron. In 1943, a field on Boca Chica Key trained aircraft carrier pilots, torpedo bombers and night fighters. In 1944, marine squadrons trained on PBJs (Marine version of the B-25 Mitchell bomber) and SBD Dauntless carrier-based dive bombers. During World War II as many as 15,000 service personnel made Key West their home. After the war ended, Meacham Field returned to civilian control and became Key West Municipal Airport.

Lake City Naval Air Station

Located on the airfield east of Lake City and established in December 1942, NAS Lake City was used during World War II to train Navy and Marine pilots in PV-1 Ventura and PV-3 Harpoon aircraft. Around 1,600 military personnel, including 200 WAVES, were stationed at the airfield during the war.

Fort Lauderdale NAS

Established on the local municipal airport in October 1942, this Naval airfield provided aircraft carrier pilot and crew training on TBF/TBM Avenger torpedo planes. The base also provided radar and air-sea rescue training. In 1943, a young Ensign George Herbert Walker Bush (later to become a U.S. President) received pilot training at NAS Fort Lauderdale.

Marianna Army Air Base

This air base in northwest Florida was a World War II pilot training facility. Training began in mid-1942 on North American AT-16 aircraft.

Marineland During WWII

Located along the Atlantic coast between St. Augustine and Daytona Beach, Marineland opened in 1938 as the world's first oceanarium. Although America's entry into World War II in December 1941, followed by gas and tire rationing that cut into tourist travel, coastal blackouts, and calls to national service for many Marineland personnel, resulted in the oceanarium's public closing, some activities continued. In the summer of 1942 the aquarium tanks were emptied and the facilities turned over to the Coast Guard for use in training combat dogs.

One wartime contribution came in the form of research that Marineland conducted under contract with the government on a shark repellent that was adopted by the U.S. Army and Navy in sea survival kits for downed personnel. Marineland scientists also developed knowledge of dolphin's sonar capabilities.

Mayport Naval Station

Located east of Jacksonville, this naval station became active in 1943 as a refueling and rearming facility for aircraft from the Jacksonville Naval Air Station. The aircraft carrier stationed here also provided actual takeoff and landing experience for pilot training. Later in World War II, the Mayport Naval Station provided gunnery and torpedo training using Corsair aircraft, anti-aircraft training, and was home port for a minesweeping group. The base was deactivated by the U.S. Navy in 1946.

The Naval Auxiliary Air Station (NAAS) Mayport was reactivated in 1948 and is the third largest fleet concentration area in the continental United States.

Melbourne Naval Air Station

Established in 1942 on the site of the Eau Gallie-Melbourne Municipal Airport, this naval air station provided flight training in F6F Hellcat, SNJ Texan, and F4F Wildcat aircraft. Peak training occurred in mid-1944 with 150 F6F Hellcats and about 1,500 naval personnel on the base. The station closed in 1946 and reverted back to the local municipality for civilian use.

Mayport Naval Station.

Mayport Naval Station.

Aircraft Carrier. Following the onset of World War II, the U.S. Navy took over the land along Ribault Bay to build a Navy base. This military installation now occupies a major part of Mayport.

MacDill Army Airfield

Established in 1941 on Tampa Bay in honor of Army aviator and World War I veteran Colonel Leslie MacDill, the 3,500-acre airfield was a major training base for the B-17 Flying Fortress, B-26 Martin Marauder, and B-29 Superfortress aircraft. As many as 15,000 military personnel were stationed here at one time during World War II. The air crews that trained at MacDill flew gallant missions in every theater of war and made an important contribution to the defeat of the Axis nations. MacDill continues to serve as a vital United States Air Force Base.

MacDill Field. Tampa's U.S. Army Air Base "MacDill Field" was an important military base during World War II. The base was later renamed MacDill Air Force Base.

MacDill Air Force Base. In 1942, young American pilots began training on B-26 medium bombers at MacDill, in Tampa. Many of the pilots trained at MacDill were sent to World War II efforts in Europe

Bombers Flying Over Tampa. This view shows bombers from MacDill Field Army Air Base flying over the Lafayette Bridge in Tampa. The minarets of the University of Tampa can be seen in the background.

Miami Beach Hotels

In early 1942, military personnel arrived in Miami Beach for training. Resort hotels became bachelor officers' quarters, enlisted men's barracks, and mess halls. By the summer of 1943, three hundred hotels and apartment buildings became military facilities in service to nearly 500,000 Army trainees. At one time, Miami Beach hotel rooms were home to 78,000 soldiers.

Miami U-Boat Attack

On May 14, 1942, in the waters off Virginia Key and Miami Beach, a German U-boat torpedoed a Mexican tanker. When the people of the Miami area saw the burning tanker, they knew that World War II was right at the area's doorstep. The sinking of the Mexican tanker *Potrero del Llano* so infuriated a then neutral Mexico that the country declared war on Germany within two weeks. The ship was struck eight miles off the Miami area coast, with a loss of thirteen Mexican lives and numerous injuries.

During 1942 and, to a lesser extent, 1943, U-boats were responsible for the torpedoing of twenty-five ships off of Florida's east coast between Daytona Beach and Key West. The Gulf Sea Frontier, a group using airplanes, blimps, and ships, was established in Miami to pursue and hound the enemy submarines. They reduced the number of ship sinkings by making the Atlantic coast and Gulf of Mexico waters inhospitable to the Germans. The Gulf Sea Frontier is also credited with sinking two German submarines.

Morrison Army Airfield

Established in 1941 on a county airfield in Palm Beach, the 1,000-man base overhauled and repaired aircraft and tested planes for airworthiness before releasing them to service. The facility was deactivated in 1947 and became Palm Beach International Airport.

Camp Murphy

This World War II Army camp served as a top-secret radar training facility. The 11,200-acre camp was named for Colonel William Herbert Murphy, a

Marching to their Classroom. In 1941, the U.S. Army invaded the tourist-oriented city of Miami Beach and turned the fancy hotels into barracks; restaurants and clubs into mess halls; churches and synagogues into classrooms; and streets, beaches and golf courses into drill practice areas. Before World War II ended, one-fourth of the Army Air Force officers and one-fifth of the enlisted men trained at Miami Beach.

U.S. Army pioneer in electronic equipment. Almost 6,000 military personnel were stationed at this facility, providing specialized radar instruction for Army, Navy and Marine Corps personnel. After the war ended, Camp Murphy became Jonathan Dickison State Park, located on the west side of Highway U.S. 1 between Stuart and Jupiter.

Fort Myers

World War II had an enormous impact on the Fort Myers area. Even before entry of the United States into World War II, signs of military preparation abounded in the area. Flying schools were established at Riddle-McKay Field at Clewiston and Dorr Field at Arcadia by the British Royal Air Force to train flyers. Several thousand military and civilian personnel served at the Page Field Air Base and the Buckingham Air Base.

Opa Locka Airport

The Opa Locka site originated in 1918 as a Navy blimp hangar. In the early 1930s a Naval Reserve Training Base was established here. In 1940 the site was designated as the Miami Naval Air Station. Training in fighter, dive-bombing and torpedo bombing took place on the base. Aircraft used on the base included SBD Dauntless dive-bombers, Brewster F2A Buffalo fighters, TBF Avenger torpedo planes, and F4F Wildcat fighters. By 1945, the base reached a peak complement of 103,000 military and civilian personnel. During the 1950s the site was used by the 3rd Marine Corps Air Wing.

Operation Pastorius

This was the code name given by Nazi Germany to the only major espionage mission conducted in the continental United States during World War II. On June 17, 1942, a German submarine U-584 surfaced at Ponte Vedra, about seven miles south of Jacksonville Beach, to unload four saboteurs. The Germans changed clothes and took a bus to downtown Jacksonville. There they registered in the Mayflower and Seminole hotels. Two members of a second German team of saboteurs, who landed in New York, betrayed the operation to the FBI. Within a week all were apprehended, tried, and convicted. The informers went to prison and the others were executed.

Orlando Army Air Base

Orlando Municipal Airport was taken over by the military in 1940 when the Army Air Corps arrived to set up a training field there. During World War II, the Orlando Army Air Base served as home for bomber and fighter groups. The base grew rapidly during the early years of the war. Thousands of troops were stationed here and dozens of buildings were quickly erected.

In 1941, the Army established a second Orlando air base in Pine Castle. The Pine Castle Army Air Field

Flexible Gunnery School. During World War II the Flexible Gunnery School was located at the Buckingham Army Air Field, east of Fort Myers in Buckingham. Here thousands of military personnel were trained on turret and waist guns on Army Air Force bombers.

Orlando Air Base. The main entrance to Orlando Air Base, manned by armed sentries in keeping with universal wartime restrictions, keynotes the striking eye appeal of this Army air base. Hundreds of native palms and brilliant flowers make this air base one of the most attractive Army posts in Florida.

Post Chapel at Orlando Air Base. A unique feature of the Post Chapel is the location of the steeple. Planes zoom low over this building as they approach and take off from the nearby flying field, necessitating the location of the steeple on the ground and to the side of the chapel.

was renamed McCoy Air Force Base in 1958 in honor of Colonel N.W. "Mike" McCoy. The Air Force vacated the airport in 1974. This site became McCoy Jetport and in 1982 Orlando International Airport.

Page Field Airport

Located in Fort Myers and leased in 1942 by the Army Air Force, this airport was originally named for Captain Richard Channing Page, a World War I hero. The Third Air Force operated a training facility at this base. B-24 bombers were used for training and to patrol for submarines over the Gulf of Mexico. Airplanes used for pilot fighter training included P-39 Airacobras, P-40 Warhawks, P-47 Thunderbolts, and P-51 Mustangs. During the height of training during World War II a complement of 4,000 personnel were stationed at this facility. After the war ended, the facility was returned to civilian use.

Pensacola Naval Air Station

The Naval Air Station in Pensacola has been recognized as the "Cradle of Naval Aviation" and "Annapolis of the Air" in recognition of its role in the history of aviation. It is one of the country's principal Naval Air Stations.

First constructed in 1826 as a U.S. Navy Yard five miles south of Pensacola. The yard closed in 1911. In 1914 the Navy's first Aeronautic Center opened on the site of the abandoned Navy Yard. As the naval aviation training facility during World War I, NAS Pensacola in 1918 carried a complement of almost 6,000 military personnel. By the end of World War I, 1,000 seaplane and hydroplane aviators had been trained at this facility.

When World War II started in 1941, flight instruction increased to 2,500 students per month. NAS Pensacola played an important role in the Navy's war efforts. Flight training was provided on several aircraft, including OS2U Kingfishers and PBY Catalinas. NAS Pensacola also provided training in photography, aviation medicine and aircraft maintenance. By the end of World War II over 28,000 naval aviators had been trained at this facility. Since the first flight training class in 1914, over 120,000 pilots have earned their wings at Pensacola. In 1976, NAS Pensacola was designated a National Historic Landmark.

Student Officers Quarters.

Annapolis of the Air. Pensacola is the home of the Naval Air Station, "Annapolis of the Air." Eglin Field is near Pensacola. During World War II it was the world's largest Proving Grounds of the Army Flying Forces, as flight training was provided on several aircraft.

National Museum of Naval Aviation. In addition to military aircraft, the museum, located on Pensacola NAS, contains many additional dramatic exhibits, including excellent paintings of World War II Navy and Marine air battles. The museum houses a collection of 180 aircraft once used by the U.S. Navy, Marines and Coast Guard.

Navy Planes Over Pensacola. During WWII the skies over Pensacola were often filled with student pilots during training exercises.

Perry Army Airfield

A sub-base to the Dale Mabry Airfield in Tallahassee, Perry became operational in June 1943. This 862-acre, World War II site provided pilot training using P-51 Mustang, P-47 Thunderbolts, and P-40 Warhawk aircraft. The airfield reverted back to civilian use after World War II.

Pinellas Army Airfield

Established on the Pinellas County Municipal Airport in 1942, this airfield provided training for fighter pilots and air crews on P-51 Mustang and P-40 Warhawk aircraft. After World War II the site became the St. Petersburg-Clearwater International Airport.

POW Camps in Florida

During World War II, more than 9,000 German prisoners were held at twenty-two Florida POW (Prisoner of War) Camps, many at or near military bases:

Elgin Field ~ Drew Field ~ DeLand ~ Camp Gordon Johnson ~ MacDill Field ~ Leesburg ~ Telogia ~ Orlando ~ Dade City ~ Dale Mabry Field ~ Winter Haven ~ Page Field ~ Camp Blanding ~ Liberty Point ~ Kendall ~ Green Cove Springs ~ Belle Glade ~ Homestead

German POWs. These prisoners were up for roll call at Jacksonville Naval Air Station.

Punta Gorda Army Airfield

This auxiliary field to the Sarasota Army Air Base was established in 1943 on the Charlotte County Airport. It was used for pilot training on P-40 Warhawk, P-47 Thunderbolt, and P-51 Mustang fighter aircraft.

Riddle Field

Located six miles northwest of Clewiston, the field was used by the McCay-Riddle Aeronautical College, a private flight school, to provide training for American and British pilots during World War II. Over 1,300 British cadets learned to fly at Riddle Field.

Sanford Naval Air Station

This World War II airbase was established in November 1942, training pilots in flying FM-1 Wildcat and F6F Hellcat carrier-based aircraft, and PBO Hudson, PV-1 Venturas, and SNB aircraft. Gunnery, bombing, and navigational technique training also occurred at this airbase.

The Navy trained half of all its pilots who fought the Japanese in World War II at the Sanford Naval Air Station. In 1945, German prisoners of war appeared in Sanford to work at the air station. The base closed at the end of the war, however, the Navy returned during the Korean and Vietnam wars, turning the airfield into a home base for nuclear bombers and reconnaissance jets, for seventeen years. In the 1960s, pilots were trained on Vigilantes for service in the Vietnam War. Eighteen Vigilantes were shot down during this war. The Sanford Naval Air Station was closed in 1968 and the airfield eventually became the Sanford/Orlando International Airport. A restored Vigilante is on display at this airport.

Sarasota Army Airfield

Established in 1942 on the Sarasota Bradenton Airport, this World War II airbase provided pilot training on B-17 Flying Fortress bombers and P-39 Airacobra fighter aircraft. After the war the site became the Sarasota Bradenton International Airport.

Saufley Field

The NAAS (Naval Auxiliary Air Station) Saufley Field was established in 1940 as an auxiliary field to the Pensacola Naval Air Station and named in honor of Lieutenant Junior Grade Richard Caswell Saufley, a naval aviator who died in 1916 in an airplane crash off Santa Rosa Island. The auxiliary field provided pilot training on SNJ Texan and Link trainers. In 1944 NAAS Saufley Field had a complement of 1,800 personnel.

St. Augustine Lighthouse

This lighthouse first saw use in 1874. During World War II the United States Coast Guard stationed armed lookouts at the site, keeping one man on watch at the top of the tower at all times. The beacon's light was dimmed to prevent friendly ships from being silhouetted in the beam, when German U-boats patrolled the Atlantic coast. A World War II Coast Guard barracks building on site serves as offices and an archaeology laboratory.

Tyndall Army Airbase

Named in honor of World War I flying ace and Florida native, Lieutenant Frank B. Tyndall, and established in 1941 along the Gulf of Mexico near Panama City, this 28,000-acre site was used primarily for B-17 Flying Fortress and B-24 Liberator gunnery training. Hollywood movie idol Clark Gable, Detroit Tiger Hank Greenberg, and thousands of airmen received gunnery schooling at this base. After World War II ended in 1945, the airbase became Tyndall Air Force Base, home to the 325th Fighter Wing.

U.S.S. Florida

This battleship was launched May 12, 1910. During World War I, the *Florida* served with the British Grand Fleet and assisted in maneuvers against the German fleet. The *Florida* also served as escort to the *George Washington*, on which President Woodrow Wilson sailed to France to promulgate the Treaty of Versailles officially ending the war. She was decommissioned in April 1931 and scrapped a year later.

Venice Army Airfield

This 1,600-acre airfield was established by the U.S. Army in 1942 and had a complement of more than 4,000 personnel whose purpose was to train maintenance personnel. Factory-staffed engine schools from Pratt, Republic, Rollison and Rolls-Royce were operated at the base. Aircraft based at this base included P-39 Airacobras, P-40s, P-47 Thunderbolts, and P-51 Mustangs. After the conclusion of World War II, the site became Venice Municipal Airport.

Vero Beach Naval Air Station

Established at a small municipal airport in 1942 to train Navy and Marine aviators, the base was used as a Marine Air Squadron Base and as a training facility for SB2A Buccaneer, F6F Hellcat, F4F/FM-1 Wildcat, and F7F Tigercat pilots. In 1944, the base provided night fighter training using F6F Hellcat and F7F Tigercat aircraft. Over 237,100 hours of flight time occurred at this base between 1942 and the base closing in 1946. After World War II, the site became the Vero Beach Municipal Airport and is home to Piper Aircraft Corporation. A Florida Historic marker about this facility is located at the airport.

Whiting Field NAS

Established in July 1943 as an auxiliary to the Pensacola Naval Air Station, the field, which took its name from Navy aviator Captain Kenneth Whiting, was constructed on 2,920 acres of agricultural land in Milton. Whiting's complement of over 3,000 personnel trained students using PBY Catalina's, SNBs (military version of the Beech Model 18 twin-engine trainer) and SNJs (Navy version of the AT-6 Texan trainer).

World War II Prisoners

During World War II, about 378,000 German and Italian prisoners were sent to prisoner of war (POW) camps throughout the United States. More than 9,000 of these prisoners were eventually incarcerated in Florida. The two major POW camps were Camp Blanding, near Starke, and Camp Gordon Johnston, near Carrabelle. There were also twenty other POW camps in Florida.

Women's Army Corps

During World War II some 272,000 women, including many Floridians, joined the Women's Army Corps. The Army established a major training facility for the WACs at Daytona Beach, where some 40,000 women eventually trained.

WAC Train at Daytona Beach.

ZEPHYRHILLS ARMY AIRFIELD

Established in 1942 at the Zephyrhills Municipal Airport, the airfield was a training base for North American P-51 Mustang fighters. Pilots who trained at this airfield saw duty over Normandy during the June 1944 Allied invasion of Europe.

6

More Fortifications and Conflicts

This chapter discusses other wars and conflicts where Floridians have served, fought and died for Florida and country: The Spanish-American War in 1898, and in more recent times, the conflicts in Korea, Vietnam, Iraq and Afghanistan.

Fort Clinch During the Spanish-American War

From 1869 until 1898 the Army maintained the reservation on caretaker status. In early 1898, the explosion and sinking of the *U.S.S. Maine* in Havana harbor thrust the U.S. into war with Spain and brought Fort Clinch to life again. Battery "A" of the 6th Artillery arrived to find Fort Clinch in a deteriorated condition. The drawbridge was rotting, sand blocked the entrance, and the site lacked drinking water and sanitation facilities. The soldiers repaired the damage and built the mount for an eight-inch breechloading rifle. All troops were removed from Fort Clinch in September 1898.

Coastal Forts

Maritime nations have long relied upon the permanent placement of weaponry to ward off attacks from the sea. This strategy protected harbors, inlets, rivers, inland territory and harbor traffic, and supported naval defense power. To mount these weapons and to house and protect the troops needed to operate and maintain them, coastal forts were built. They were designed and constructed to conform to surrounding terrain and to the nature of the perceived threat. More than anything, forts were built in response to weapons technology. The location of a fort and the height and thickness of its walls had to repel whatever artillery could be fired from ships. The development of aerial bombing in World War I made most forts obsolete.

The first coastal forts in colonial Florida were made of earth or wood — plentiful materials at hand for quick construction and defense — and were positioned to warn off competing claimants to Florida. These forts were effective against Native Americans, but were generally inadequate against attacks by other Europeans. Later forts were built of masonry, brick, and reinforced concrete and were designed to defend settlements, ports, or naval installations.

Some of Florida's coastal forts have disappeared while others are preserved as they originally were built. Many existing forts are located within national and state parks or wildlife refuges. They have undergone refurbishing or rebuilding in order to provide us with a glimpse of our maritime past.

Camp Cuba Libre

This temporary Spanish-American War training post was located at Jacksonville. By September 1898 around 29,000 soldiers were stationed at the camp. The soldiers outnumbered the local populace, and their free-wheeling, free-spending presence gave the city a carnival atmosphere.

Fort Dade (Egmont Key)

In 1898, when war with Spain seemed certain, the people of Tampa petitioned Congress to build fortifications at the mouth of Tampa Bay for their protection. Fort Dade was built on Egmont Key, thirty-five miles southwest of Tampa. The 378-acre Fort Dade was named in honor of Major Francis L. Dade who was killed with almost his entire command by Seminole Indians in 1835.

Fort Dade had an artillery garrison aggregating six officers and one hundred fifty-four men. The main armament for the fort included two 8-inch guns, two Armstrong rapid fire 6-inch guns, one 12-pound brass cannon, three rapid-fire 15-pounders, two 10-inch disappearing guns, and several batteries of 10-inch and 14-inch guns. A narrow gauge railroad was built to serve and connect all of the gun positions.

Fort Dade was an embarkation point for Lt. Colonel Teddy Roosevelt and his Rough Riders; it was also a quarantine camp for returning troops during the Spanish-American War.

Desert Shield/ Desert Storm Operation

Seventeen Florida National Guard units, from twelve different cities were federalized for Operation Desert Shield/Desert Storm. A total of 1,790 Florida Guardsmen served in the conflict; 1,589 Army Guardsmen were mobilized and joined by 105 Army National Guard and 96 Air National Guard volunteers.

Several of the units were sent to Kuwait, Saudi Arabia and Iraq and performed many duties including maintenance, engineering, ordnance, medical, and military police. The last Florida National Guard unit returned home on August 14, 1991.

Fort DeSoto

In 1898, the United States became involved in a conflict in Cuba which led to the Spanish-American War. This event prompted the citizens of Tampa to demand military defenses for Tampa Bay. Henry B. Plant, a prominent railroad, shipping and hotel magnate, was instrumental in convincing the Secretary of War to order construction of fortifications on Mullet and Egmont Keys. Because of its close proximity to Cuba and port facilities, Tampa became the port of embarkation for troops and supplies going to the Caribbean war zones.

Named after Spanish explorer Hernando DeSoto, Fort DeSoto was built between 1898 and 1903 on Mullet Key to protect the entrance to Tampa Bay. Along with Fort Dade on Egmont Key, it was used primarily during the Spanish-American War.

Geronimo Imprisoned in Pensacola

In 1886, Geronimo, a brilliant military leader of the Apache Indians, surrendered to the U.S. Army and was imprisoned at Fort Barrancas in Pensacola. Visitors from all over the world came to see the once feared warrior. Geronimo who became, for a time, Pensacola's number one tourist attraction. Geronimo's wife Ga-ha died during internment and was buried at Barrancas National Cemetery.

Geronimo—Apache Indian Leader.

Mortar Pit at Fort DeSoto. The two twelve-inch Seacoast Mortars were located in a Battery Laidley Mortar Pit at Fort DeSoto. These mortars stood ready to defend the harbor of Tampa Bay, but never fired a shot at an enemy. Artillery spotters in towers, would have directed the firing of these weapons.

Fort Jefferson

Sixty-eight miles west of Key West, lies a cluster of seven islands (Loggerhead Key, Garden Key, Bush Key, Long Key, Hospital Key, Middle Key and East Key), composed of coral reefs and sand, called the Dry Tortugas.

Poised to protect the Tortugas was one of the largest forts ever built. Nearly thirty years in the making (1846-1875), Fort Jefferson was never finished nor fully armed, yet it was a vital link in the chain of coastal forts. Fort Jefferson, the most sophisticated of the coastal forts, was a brilliant and undeniable symbol that the United States wanted to be left alone. Though never attacked, the fort fulfilled its intended role. It helped to protect the peace and prosperity of a young nation.

The hexagon-shaped Fort Jefferson was seven-eighths of a mile in perimeter and covered most of the 16 acres of Garden Key. The outside walls were 8 feet thick and each of the hexagonal sides 450 feet long and 50 feet high. The massive foundations rested on coral rock 10 feet below sea level. It is estimated that 16 million bricks were used in building the fort. Within the fort's court were three-story officer and enlisted men's quarters and powder magazines.

The fort had three gun tiers, designed to mount 450 cannons, and a garrison of 1,500 men. The guns were located so that 125 of them could simultaneously zero in on the same target. Only 243 cannons were actually mounted on the fortification and not one of them was ever fired.

Aerial View of Fort Jefferson. The six-sided Fort Jefferson on Garden Key in Dry Tortugas, sixty-eight miles west of Key West, is the largest of the massive brick fortifications built during the nineteenth century for the defense of the American coast.

Fort Jefferson Bastions.
The massive tower bastions are the largest ever constructed in America.

Fort Jefferson.
Construction began in 1846 and continued until 1875, but the fort was never entirely finished. This six-sided three-tiered casemated fortress was designed for a garrison of 7,500 men and an armament of 450 cannons.

Hot Shot Furnace. The large hot shot furnace, shown in the foreground, was designed to heat cannonballs red hot. The cannonballs were then fired at wooden ships in hopes of setting them on fire. As metal warships replaced wooden ships this type of furnace became obsolete. The officer's quarters and foundation for the enlisted men's barracks are shown in the background.

View of the Terreplein with a 10-inch Coast Artillery Cannon.

Inside Fort Jefferson. The extensive, open parade of Fort Jefferson is complemented by two tiers of casemates and a tier of barbette cannons. The size of the fort is overwhelming to the visitor.

View of the Parade Ground from Lighthouse.

Fort Jefferson Construction. It is estimated that 16 million bricks were used in building Fort Jefferson. The outside walls were 8 feet thick, 450 feet long and 50 feet high.

Fort Jefferson Armament. Fort Jefferson was designed to be the most heavily armed fortification in the United States, mounting 450 cannons. While the fort never reached this level of armament, it served its role as a fort and later as a coaling station with a grandeur not matched by any other fortification.

Powder Magazine.

View of Sally Port and Drawbridge — Only Entrance to Fort Jefferson.

Fort Jefferson Casemates.
The incredible size of Fort Jefferson makes the classic photograph of arches diminishing in the distance especially impressive. The casemates had a set of arches between the cannons, and a second set of arches for communication behind the extreme of the carriage. These arches provided access to the Rodman cannons.

Fort Jefferson Lighthouse.
The Tortugas Harbor Light, constructed of black boiler-plate iron and erected in 1876, sits atop the massive walls of Fort Jefferson. The structure replaced the original brick Tortugas Lighthouse which was built in 1825, shortly after Florida became a U.S. Territory

Reaching Fort Jefferson. Sixty-eight miles west of Key West is Dry Tortugas archipelago and Fort Jefferson, a hexagonal fort that is among the largest brick-and-masonry structures in the Western Hemisphere. The fort can be reached by either boat or seaplane from Key West.

Jupiter Lighthouse

This lighthouse first lit up the shallow waters off the Jupiter Inlet July 10, 1860. Distracted by Seminole Indian attacks, the soldiers took six years to build the 105-foot tall structure. During the Civil War, the Confederates hid the lighting mechanism until after the war. During World War II, the lighthouse was used as a secret listening post monitoring messages with a priority on locating German submarines.

Korean Conflict

The Korean Conflict of 1950-1953 was the most important war ever fought between the West and Communism. It saw sixteen armies from all five continents deployed under U.S. command and the U.N. flag against two armies, those of North Korea and China. It brought the people of Korea destruction, devastation and tragedy; there were millions of deaths and more millions of divided families. Yet it is still a little known conflict; both sides claim to have won, yet both actually seem to feel they lost. During this war 972 men of the Florida National Guard were called to active duty. In addition to these, 27,823 Floridians were drafted and 84,257 voluntarily enlisted. *(The author served with the 1st Marine Division in Korea during 1951-1952.)*

Mexican War

Floridians have fought in this country's wars ever since volunteers formed five companies to fight in the War with Mexico in 1846-1848, the year after Florida became a state. Fifty-five of the Mexican War soldiers died of disease and one was killed in action.

Camp Miami

This temporary Spanish-American War Army post was established in 1898 in the downtown Miami area. The encampments for 7,000 soldiers were situated on the Royal Palm Hotel grounds, on the north shore of the Miami River.

Orlando Naval Training Center

On June 30, 1968, the Orlando Air Force Base was turned over to the U.S. Navy and the site became the Orlando Naval Training Center. Along with recruits, NTC trained specialists in electronics, navigation, nuclear propulsion and other skills. At any given time, at the peak of activities, there were around 18,000 personnel on the

Orlando Naval Training Center.

base. The Naval Training Center was closed, in phases, during 1994 and 1998.

Fort Pickens After the Civil War

From 1886 until 1888 (nineteen months), Geronimo, the Apache Indian Chief, and several of his band of warriors were held prisoners in Fort Pickens. One of Geronimo's wives is buried at the Barrancas National Cemetery across the bay in the Naval Air Station.

Between 1890 and 1900, Fort Pickens was modernized and strengthened. At the beginning of the Spanish-American War in 1898, Fort Pickens again was pressed into service as an active defense fortification and long-range coastal guns were mounted.

Persian Gulf War

In 1990 the Middle Eastern country of Iraq, led by its president Saddam Hussein, suddenly invaded Kuwait, its much smaller neighbor. Iraqi troops took control of Kuwait's capital, seized the country's rich oil fields, and forced the Kuwaiti royal family into exile.

The United States and the United Nations were forced to use military force against Iraq. The short, but decisive, war, beginning on January 16, 1991, destroyed Iraq's industrial and war-making facilities, crushed most of the Iraqi army, and liberated Kuwait, all in just forty-three days.

This war was the first time Floridians and other Americans were able to watch the war on an hourly basis — it was the world's first "real-time television war."

Again, in 2003, U.N. forces, led by U.S. troops, destroyed Iraq military control and freed the Iraqi people from their cruel leader, Saddam Hussein.

Several thousand personnel in Florida's National Guard units were involved in many capacities during military operations in the Persian Gulf conflicts. Many Florida Soldiers and Marines are still serving their country in Afghanistan and Iraq.

Prisoners at Fort Marion

An important service of Fort Marion was as a military prison. Between September 8, 1837 and October 27, 1838, nine Seminole Indian leaders, eighty-one warriors, and an unknown number of women and children were imprisoned at Fort Marion (Castillo de San Marcos). On May 21, 1875, seventy-four Plains Indians arrived at Fort Marion to be

Prisoners at Fort Marion (Castillo de San Marcos).

imprisoned for the next three years. Between April 16, 1886 and November 7, 1887, over 500 Apache Indians arrived at Fort Marion as prisoners of war. The last real military use of the fort was a prison during the Spanish-American War.

Spanish-American War

At the end of the nineteenth century, America became involved in a short war. The Spanish-American War began in 1898 and lasted only three months. There was much unrest between America and Cuba. During this unrest the American battleship *U.S.S. Maine* was mysteriously blown up in the Havana harbor. Shortly

Soldiers at Port Tampa. During the Spanish-American War, thousands of soldiers were set to Tampa for possible deployment to Cuba.

Soldiers at Camp Miami During Spanish-American War.

after the sinking of the *Maine*, the United States declared war on Spain. Florida immediately became the grounds of military activities.

Forts were built around gaping Tampa Bay as a defense against attacks from Cuba. Military training camps were established in Jacksonville, Tampa, Fernandina Lakeland and Miami. Tampa became the principal port of embarkation to Cuba. Colonel Theodore (Teddy) Roosevelt stationed 30,000 of his Rough Riders in Tampa. Roosevelt and his soldiers were to go to Cuba and put an end to the war. Florida's militia never made it to Cuba because the fighting had lasted only a few months.

St. Johns Bluff Fortification

In 1898 Jacksonville became a major staging area for the Spanish-American War, and around 29,000 soldiers were stationed at "Camp Cuba Libre" in the city. The Army built a defensive gun battery at St. Johns Bluff which overlooked the St. Johns River. Railroad tracks were installed and a tram was used to haul the artillery and ammunition to the top of the bluff. Guns were mounted on disappearing carriages that retracted the barrels below concrete parapets for loading purposes, thus protecting the gunners. The battery also featured large metal doors and an underground bombproof ammunition magazine.

Fort Zachary Taylor

In 1898 the Army modified Fort Zachary Taylor in Key West to improve the coastal defense system. They removed the top two tiers of the fort and built two new batteries, Osceola and Adair, and placed heavier weaponry upon them. The project was finished just as the Spanish-American War was ending.

U.S.S. Maine

In 1898, unrest in Havana led President William McKinley to dispatch the *U.S.S. Maine* to Cuba to show the flag and protect Americans and American interests. The American warship steamed into Havana harbor on January 25 and was moored in an area reserved for warships. On February 15 an explosion ripped through the *Maine*'s hull, taking 266 lives and sparking a crisis that swiftly led to the Spanish-American War.

***U.S.S. Maine* in Havana Harbor.**

***Maine* Monument.**
This monument in Key West was erected in memory of the victims of the disaster of the U.S. Battleship *U.S.S. Maine* in Havana Harbor, February 15, 1898.

VIETNAM WAR

In 1945, Ho Chi Minh proclaimed Vietnamese independence. From 1946 to 1954, the French opposed independence, and Ho Chi Minh led guerrilla warfare against them. It ended with a Vietnamese victory in 1954. An agreement was signed at Geneva, Switzerland in 1954, providing for a temporary division of the country between a Communist-dominated north and a U.S.-supported south. Activities of pro-Communist rebels in South Vietnam led to U.S. intervention and war (1965-1975), which caused great destruction and loss of life. It came to a brief halt in 1973, when a cease-fire agreement was signed (January 27) and U.S. troops were withdrawn. The war was soon resumed. In 1975 the South Vietnamese government collapsed and was replaced by a regime dominated by the Communists.

During the Vietnam War one Florida National Guard unit was called to active duty; 40,352 Floridians were drafted into military service; and 146,028 voluntarily enlisted. Florida casualties were 1,897 during this war.

Vietnam War Encampment Display at Camp Blanding Museum.

References and Selected Reading

Literature pertaining to the military history of Florida exists in such abundance that any bibliography seeking to be comprehensive would fill at least a sizable volume, if not more. Primary source materials may be found in a variety of forms and include letters, diaries, journals, reports and unpublished manuscripts. These materials may be found in a variety of repositories ranging from state archives to various university and regional historical society libraries.

Newspapers and periodicals also contain a wealth of material on military topics. Many Florida historical societies regularly publish a journal or newsletter, many of which contain articles relevant to research on Florida military topics.

In the bibliography that follows, no attempt was made to be all-inclusive. Nevertheless, there was a conscientious effort to control as much ground as deemed appropriate and practical given the necessary limitations of space. In any event, this list of selected books and pamphlets will guide the reader toward other works that may shed further light on topics of particular interest. There are many more specialized titles available, covering particular forts, events, battles, armament, people, and other related topics.

Although some of the older titles, many of them classics in the field, are now out of print, they can be found in library collections.

Abbey, Kathryn Trimmer. *Florida: Land of Change*. Chapel Hill, North Carolina: University of North Carolina Press, 1941.

Adams, William R. and Paul L. Weaver, III. *Historic Places of St. Augustine and St. Johns County*. St. Augustine, Florida: Southern Heritage Press, 1993.

A Heritage Revisited. Tallahassee, Florida: Bicentennial Commission of Florida, 1976.

Alger, Russell A. *The Spanish-American War*. New York, New York: Harper & Bros., 1901.

Arana, Luis Rafael and Albert Manucy. *The Building of Castillo de San Marcos*. St. Augustine, Florida: Eastern National Park & Monument Association, 1977.

Arnade, Charles W. *The Siege of St. Augustine in 1702*. Gainesville, Florida: University of Florida Press, 1959.

Arsenault, Raymond. *St. Petersburg and The Florida Dream, 1888-1950*. Gainesville, Florida: University Press of Florida 1996.

Athearn, Robert G. *The New World*. New York, New York: Dell Publishing Company, 1963.

Back to the Water. Tallahassee, Florida: Florida Department of Community Affairs, 1986.

Ball, Jim, Roz Foster, Douglas Hendriksen and Vera Zimmerman. *History of Brevard County, Volume 3*. Cocoa, Florida: Brevard County Historical Commission, 2001.

Baltzell, George F. *Battle of Olustee*. Melbourne, Florida: Florida Historical Quarterly, No. 4 (1931).

Bane, Michael and Mary Ellen Moore. *Tampa: Yesterday, Today & Tomorrow*. Tampa, Florida: Mishler and King Publishing, 1981.

Bears, Edwin C. *Fort Barrancas: Gulf Islands National Seashore*. Washington D.C.: National Park Service, 1980.

Belleville, Bill. *River of Lakes: A Journey on Florida's St. Johns River*. Athens, Georgia: University of Georgia Press, 2000.

Bemrose, John. *Reminiscences of the Second Seminole War*. Dade City, Florida: Seminole Wars Historic Foundation, 2001.

Bennett, Charles E. *Fort Caroline and Its Leader*. Gainesville, Florida: University of Florida Press, 1976.

Laudonniere and Fort Caroline. Gainesville, Florida: University of Florida Press, 1964.

Bense, Judith A. *Archaeology of Colonial Pensacola*. Gainesville, Florida: University of Florida Press, 1999.
Pensacola Archaeological Survey, Volume 1. Pensacola, Florida: Pensacola Archaeological Society, 1989.

Bergen, Bernice Brooks. *Sarsota Times Past: A Reflective Collection of the Florida Gulf Coast*. Miami, Florida: Valiant Press, 1993.

Bice, David A. *A Panorama of Florida*. Marceline, Missouri: Walsworth Publishing Company, 1989.

Bickel, Karl A. *The Mangrove Coast*. New York, New York: Coward-McCann, Inc., 1942.

Billinger, Jr., Robert D. *Hitler's Soldiers in The Sunshine State*. Gainesville, Florida: University Press of Florida, 2000.

Blakey, Arch Fredric. *Parade of Memories*. Green Cove Springs, Florida: Clay County Bicentennial Steering Committee, 1976.

Bockelman, Charles W. *Six Columns and Fort New Smyrna*. Daytona Beach, Florida: Halifax Historical Society, 1985.

Borremans, Nina. *Fort Mose: A Free Black Community*. Tallahassee, Florida: Department of State, 1996.

Boyd, Mark F., Hale G. Smith and John W. Griffin. *Here They Once Stood*. Gainesville, Florida: University of Florida Press, 1951.

Brevard, Caroline Mays. *A History of Florida*. New York, New York: American Book Company, 1904.

Brown, Jennifer D. *Castillo de San Marcos National Monument Historic Resource Study*. Atlanta, Georgia: National Park Service, 1997.

Bullen, Adelaide K. *Florida Indians of Past and Present*. Delray Beach, Florida: Southern Publishing Company, 1965.

Burt, Jesse and Robert B. Ferguson. *Indians of the South East: Then and Now*. New York, New York: Abingdon Press, 1973.

Cardwell, Sr., Harold D., editor. *The Civil War in Volusia County*. Daytona Beach, Florida: Halifax Historical Society, 1987.

Cardwell, Sr., Harold D. and Priscilla D. Cardwell. *Port Orange: A Great Community, Vol. 1*. Port Orange, Florida: City of Port Orange, 2001.

Carr, Robert S., editor. *The Battle of Okeechobee*. Miami, Florida: Archaaeological & Historical Conservancy, 1987.

Carter, Alden R. *The War of 1812*. New York, New York: Franklin Watts, 1992.

Castillo de San Marcos. St. Augustine, Florida: Century Souvenir Company, 1981.

Castillo de San Marcos: A Brief History. St. Augustine, Florida: Century Souvenir Company, 1992.

Castillo de San Marcos: Official National Park Handbook. Washington D.C.: National Park Service, 1993.

Chorlian, Meg, editor. *St. Augustine: America's Oldest City*. Peterborough, New Hampshire: Cobblestone Publishing Company, 1995.

Clarke, Mary Helm. *South Florida Treasure Trails*. Tallahassee, Florida: Key Publishing Company, 1949.

Clayton, Laurence A., Vernon James Knight, Jr., and Edward C. Moore, editors. *The DeSoto Chronicles: The Expedition of Hernando de Soto to North America 1539-1543*. Tuscaloosa, Alabama: University of Alabama Press.

Cole, John W. *Pictorial History of Pensacola: City of Five Flags*. Pensacola, Florida: Fiesta of the Five Flags Association, 1952.

Coles, David J. *Florida World War II Heritage Trail*. Tallahassee, Florida: Florida Department of State, 2004.
Men and Arms: Sketches of the Commanders and Units of the Olustee Campaign. Olustee, Florida: Olustee Battlefield Citizens Support Organization, 1995.
The Battle of Olustee. Olustee, Florida: Olustee Battlefield Citizens Support Organization, 1992.

Conly, Robert L. *St. Augustine, Nation's Oldest City, Vol. 129, No. 2*. Washington D.C.: National Geographic Society, 1966.

Connor, Jeannette Thurber, Editor. *Colonial Records of Spanish Florida, 2 volumes*. DeLand, Florida: Florida Historical Society, 1925-30.
Pedro Menendez De Aviles. Gainesville, Florida: University of Florida Press, 1964.

Corse, Carita Doggett. *Dr. Andrew Turnbull and the New Smyrna Colony of Florida*. Jacksonville, Florida: The Drew Press, 1919.
Silver Springs: Shrine of the Water Gods. Self-published, 1935.

Covington, James W. *The Billy Bowlegs War, 1855-1858: The Final Stand of the Seminoles Against the*

Whites. Chuluota, Florida: Chuluota: Micker House Publishers, 1982.

Craft, Stephen G. *Embry-Riddle At War: Aviation Training During World War II*. Gainesville, Florida: University Press of Florida, 2009.

Davis, T. Frederick. *History of Jacksonville, Florida and Vicinity 1513 to 1924*. St. Augustine, Florida: The Florida Historical Society, 1925.

Davis, William Watson, editor. *The Civil War and Reconstruction in Florida, 1913 Reprint*. Gainesville, Florida: University of Florida Press, 1964.

Deagan, Kathleen and Darcie MacMahon. *Fort Mose: Colonial America's Black Fortress of Freedom*. Gainesville, Florida: University Press of Florida, 1995.

DeQuesada, Alejandro M. *World War II in Tampa Bay*. Dover, New Hampshire: Arcadia Publishing, 1997.

DeReparaz, Carmen. *I Alone: Bernardo de Galvez and the Taking of Pensacola in 1781*. Madrid, Spain: Ediciones de Cultura Hispanica, 1993.

Dewhurst, William W. *The History of St. Augustine, Florida*. New York, New York: G. P. Putnam's Sons, 1885.

Dictionary of Florida Historic Places, Volumes 1 & 2. St. Clair Shores, Michigan: Somerset Publishers, 1991.

Dickison, Mary Elizabeth. *Dickison and His Men: Reminiscences of the War in Florida (1890)*. Gainesville, Florida: University of Florida Press, 1962.

Dunn, Hampton. *Tampa: A Pictorial History*. Norfolk, Virginia: Donning Company, 1985.

Eby, Cecil D., editor. *Memoir of a West Pointer in Saint Augustine, 1824-1826*. St. Augustine, Florida: Saint Augustine Historical Society, 1964.

Edwards, Virginia. *Stories of Old St. Augustine*. St. Augustine, Florida: St. Augustine Historical Society, 1971.

Elliott, John Huxtable. *Spain and Its World 1500-1700*. New Haven, Connecticut:: Yale University Press, 1999.

Ellsworth, Lucius and Linda Ellsworth. *Pensacola: The Deep Water City*. Tulsa, Oklahoma: Continental Heritage Press, 1982.

Ervin, William, William R. *The Seminole War: Prelude to Victory 1823-1838*. Holly Hill, Florida: W. & S. Ervin Publishing, 1983.

Fairbanks, George R. *The History and Antiquities of the City of St. Augustine, Florida*. New York, New York: Charles B. Norton, 1858.

Federal Works Agency. *Miami and Dade County*. Northport, New York: Bacon, Percy and Daggett Publishers, 1941.

Federal Writers' Project. *Florida: A Guide to the Southernmost State*. New York, New York: Oxford University Press, 1939.

Seeing St. Augustine. St. Augustine, Florida: The Record Company, 1937.

Florida Black Heritage Trail. Tallahassee, Florida: Florida Department of State, 1994.

Florida Historical Quarterly, The, Vol. XLIV, July-October, 1965. Tampa, Florida: Florida Historical Society, 1965.

Florida World War II Heritage Trail. Tallahassee, Florida: Division of Historical Resources, Florida Department of State, 2004.

Ford, Lawrence Carroll. *The Triangular Struggle for Spanish Pensacola, 1689-1739*. Washington, D.C.: The Catholic University of America Press, 1939.

Fort Barrancas 1875. Pensacola, Florida: Pensacola Historical Society, 1998.

Fort Caroline. Jacksonville, Florida: Jacksonville Historical Society.

Fort Matanzas National Monument. St. Augustine, Florida: U.S. Department of the Interior, 1995.

Francke, Jr., Arthur E. *Early Days of Seminole County*. Sanford, Florida: Seminole County Historical Commission, 1984.

Fort Mellon 1837-42: A Microcosm of the Second Seminole War. Miami, Florida: Banyan Books, Inc. 1977.

Frank, Andrew K. *The Routledge Historical Atlas of the American South*. New York, New York: Routledge, 1999.

Freitus, Joseph and Anne Freitus. *Florida: The War Years 1938-1945*. Niceville, Florida: Wind Canyon Publishing, 1998.

Fretwell, Jacqueline K. editor. *Civil War Times in St. Augustine*. St. Augustine, Florida: St. Augustine Historical Society, 1988.

Fretwell, Jackqueline K. and Susan R. Parker, editors. *Clash Between Cultures: Spanish East Florida 1784-1821*. St. Augustine, Florida: St. Augustine Historical Society, 1988.

Friend, Sandra. *Florida in the Civil War: A State in Turmoil*. Brookfield, Connecticut: Twenty-First Century Books, 2001.

Gallant, Gene. *The Last Pine Tree: A Look at Florida's Seminole Wars*. Ocala, Florida: Environmental Education Center, 1993.

Gannon, Michael. *The New History of Florida*. Gainesville, Florida: University Press of Florida, 1996.

Gibbons, Faye. *Hernando De Soto: A Search for Gold and Glory*. Birmingham, Alabama: Crane Hill Publishers, 2002.

Gibson, Lillian Dillard. *Annals of Volusia: 1558-1978*. Volusia, Florida: R. Alex Gibson, 1978.

Gifford, John C. *Billy Bowlegs and the Seminole War*. Coconut Grove, Florida: The Triangle Company, 1925.

Gill, Joan E. and Beth R. Read. *Born of the Sun*. Hollywood, Florida: Worth International Communications Corporation, 1975.

Gleasner, Bill and Diana Gleasner. *RVing America's Backroads: Florida*. Agoura, California: Trailer Life Books, 1989.

Goodwin, Gary and Suzanne Walker. *Florida Black Heritage Trail*. Tallahassee, Florida: Florida Department of State, 1994.

Graff, Mary B. *Mandarin on the St. Johns*. Gainesville, Florida: University of Florida Press, 1953.

Grafton, John. *The American Revolution*. New York, New York: Dover Publications, Inc., 1975.

Halbert, H. S. and T. H. Ball. *The Creek War of 1813 and 1814*. Tuscaloosa, Alabama: University of Alabama Press.

Hann, John H. and Bonnie G. McEwan. *The Apalachee Indians and Mission San Luis*. Gainesville: University Press of Florida, 1988.

Hanna, Alfred Jackson. *Fort Maitland: Its Origin and History*. Maitland, Florida: The Fort Maitland Committee, 1936.

Hanna, Alfred Jackson and Kathryn Abbey Hanna. *Lake Okeechobee*. Indianapolis, Indiana: The Bobbs-Merrill Company, 1948.

Hardee, Suzanne Davis. *The Golden Age of Amelia Island*. Fernandina Beach, Florida: Amelia Island Museum of History, 1995.

Harman, Joyce Elizabeth. *Trade and Privateering in Spanish Florida, 1732-1763*. Tuscaloosa, Alabama: University of Alabama Press, 2004.

Harvey, Karen. *St. Augustine and St. Johns County*. Virginia Beach, Virginia: Donning Company, 1980.

Hatt, Christine. *World War I, 1914-18*. New York, New York: Franklin Watts, 2000.

Hatton, Hap. Tropical Splendor: *An Architectural History of Florida*. New York, New York: Alfred A. Knopf, 1987.

Hawk, Robert. *Florida's Army: Militia/State Troops/National Guard 1565-1985*. Englewood, New Jersey: Pineapple Press, 1986.

Heidler, David S. and Jeanne T. Heidler. *Old Hickory's War*. Mechanicsburg, Pennsylvania: Stackpole Books, 1996.

History of the Seminole Wars. Dade City, Florida: Seminole Wars Historic Foundation, 1992.

Hollingsworth, Tracy. *History of Dade County, Florida*. Self-published, 1936.

Hughes, Kenneth J. *A Chronological History of Fort Jupiter and U.S. Military Operations in the Loxahatchee Region, 1838-1858*. Fort Lauderdale, Florida: Florida Coast Research and Publishing, Inc., 1992.

Hurley, Neil E. *Lighthouses of the Dry Tortugas: An Illustrated History*. Aiea, Hawaii: Historic Lighthouse Publishers, 1994.

Irving, Theodore. *The Conquest of Florida*. New York, New York: George P. Putnam & Sons, 1851.

Jaccard, Deon L. *Clash of the Cultures*. Amelia Island, Florida: Museum of History, 1992.

Jackson, Page S. *An Informed History of St. Petersburg*. St. Petersburg, Florida: Great Outdoors Publishing Co., 1962.

Jameson, Colin G. *East Martello Tower*. Key West, Florida: Key West Art & Historical Society, 1992.

Johns, John E. *Florida During the Civil War*. Gainesville, Florida: University of Florida Press, 1963.

Jones, Kenneth M. *War With The Seminoles–1835-1842*. New York, New York: Franklin Watts, Inc., 1975.

Joyce, Edward R. *St. Francis Barracks: A Contradiction of Terms*. St. Augustine, Florida: St. Augustine Historical Society, 1989.

Keenan, Jerry. *Encyclopedia of American Indian Wars, 1492-1890*. New York, New York: W.W. Norton & Company, 1997.

Ketchum, Eleanor. *Tales of Tallahassee*. Tallahassee, Florida: Jerry Dye and Associates, 1976.

Kimball, Christopher Delano. *Timeline of Events and Battles of the Florida Seminole Wars*. Self-published, 2001.

Kleinberg, Eliot. *Historical Traveler's Guide to Florida*. Sarasota, Florida: Pineapple Press, 1997.
War In Paradise: Stories of World War II in Florida. Melbourne, Florida: Florida Historical Society Press, 1999.

Kleinberg, Howard. *Miami: The Way We Were*. Tampa, Florida: Surfside Publishing, 1989.

Knetsch, Joe. *Florida's Seminole Wars: 1817-1858*. Charleston, South Carolina: Arcadia Publishing, 2003.

Krull, Kathleen. *V Is For Victory: America Remembers World War II*. New York, New York: Alfred A. Knopf, Inc., 1995.

Landers, Jane. *Fort Mose*. St. Augustine, Florida: St. Augustine Historical Society, 1992.

Landrum, L. Wayne. *Fort Jefferson and the Dry Tortugas National Park*. Big Pine Key, Florida: Self-published, 2003.

Laudonniere, Rene. *Three Voyages*. Tuscaloosa, Alabama: University of Alabama Press.

Laumer, Frank. *Dade's Last Command*. Gainesville, Florida: University Press of Florida, 1995.
Massacre! Gainesville, Florida: University of Florida Press, 1968.

Lavender, David. *De Soto, Coronado, Cabrillo: Explorers of the Northern Mystery*. Washington, D.C.: U.S. Department of the Interior, 1992.

Lawson, Edith Ridenour. *Florida Indians: Noble Redmen of the South*. St. Petersburg, Florida: Valkyrie Press, 1977.

Lawson, Sarah. *A Foothold in Florida*. West Sussex, England: Antique Atlas Publications, 1992.

Lee, Howard. *The Story of Old St. Augustine*. St. Augustine, Florida: The Record Press, 1951.

Lewis, Emanuel Raymond. *Seacoast Fortifications of the United States: An Introductory History*. Annapolis, Maryland: Naval Institute Press, 1979.

Liston, Broward. *Waves of Challenge: A History of the Daytona Beach/Halifax Area*. Dallas, Texas: Taylor Publishing Company, 1996.

Luther, Gary. *History of New Smyrna*. New Smyrna Beach, Florida: Luthers Publishing, 2001.

MacMahon, Darcie A. and William H. Marquardt. *The Calusa and Their Legacy*. Gainesville, Florida: University Press of Florida, 2004.

MacRae, Mary Isabel. *Citrus County Historical Notes*. Iverness, Florida: Citrus County Historical Society, 1993.

Mahon, John K. *History of the Second Seminole War, 1835-1842*. Gainesville, Florida: University Press of Florida, 1967.

Manucy, Albert C. *Artillery Through The Ages*. Washington, D.C.: U.S. Department of the Interior, 1949.
Florida's Menendez. St. Augustine, Florida: The St. Augustine Historical Society, 1965.
Menendez. Sarasota, Florida: Pineapple Press, 1983.
Pages from the Past: A Pictorial History of Fort Jefferson. Homestead, Florida: Florida National Parks and Monuments Association, 1999.
The Building of Castillo de San Marcos. Washington, D.C.: United States Government Printing Office, 1961.

Manuel, Dale. *Old Sea Forts Of Florida*. Del Valle, Texas: Self-published, 1997.

Marth, Del and Martha J. Marth. *The 1978 Florida Almanac*. St. Petersburg, Florida: Willow Creek, 1977.

Martin, Richard A. *Eternal Spring*. St. Petersburg, Florida: Great Outdoors Press, 1966.

Martin, Sidney Walter. *Florida During the Territorial Days*. Athens, Georgia: University of Georgia Press, 1944.

Maynard, Theodore. *DeSoto and the Conquistadores*. New York, New York: Longmans, Green & Co., 1930.

McCarthy, Kevin M. *Apalachicola Bay*. Sarasota, Florida: Pineapple Press, 2004.
Aviation in Florida. Sarasota, Florida: Pineapple Press, 2003.

McGrath, John T. *The French in Early Florida*. Gainesville, Florida: University Press of Florida, 2000.

McIver, Stuart B. *Fort Lauderdale and Broward County*. Woodland Hills, California: Windsor Publications, 1983.

McKay, John. *Civil War Sites in the Southern States*. Gulfport, Connecticut: Globe Pequot Press, 2005.

McReynolds, Edwin C. *The Seminoles*. Norman, Oklahoma: University of Oklahoma Press, 1985.

Milanich, Jerald T. and Charles Hudson. *Hernando De Soto and The Indians of Florida*. Gainesville, Florida: University Press of Florida, 1993.

Milanich, Jerald T. and Susan Milbrath, editors. *First Encounters: Spanish Explorations in the Caribbean and the United States, 1492-1570*. Gainesville, Florida: University of Florida Press, 1989.

Miller, Francis Trevelyan, editor. *The Photographic History of the Civil War: Forts and Artillery*. New York, New York: Castle Books, 1957.

Missall John and Mary Lou Missal. *The Seminole Wars: America's Longest Indian Conflict*. Gainesville, Florida: University Press of Florida, 2004.

Moore, Robert J. *Native Americans*. Edison, New Jersey: Chartwell Books, Inc., 2002.

Mooris, Allan, comp. *The Florida Handbook. Twenty-ninth biennial editions to date*. Tallahassee, Florida: Peninsular Publishing Company, 1947-2004.

Mueller, Edward A. *Steamboating on The St. Johns*. Melbourne, Florida: South Brevard Historical Society, 1980.

Muir, Jr., Thomas and David P. Ogden. *The Fort Pickens Story*. Pensacola, Florida: Pensacola Historical Society, 1989.

Mulder, Kenneth W. *Seminoles: Days of Long Ago*. Tampa, Florida: Mulder Enterprises, 1991.

National Museum of Naval Aviation: The Aircraft Collection. Pensacola, Florida: The Flight Deck Store, 2004.

Neill, Winfred T. *The Story of Florida's Seminole Indians*. St. Petersburg, Florida: Great Outdoors Publishing Company, 1956.

Nulty, William H. *Confederate Florida: The Road to Olustee*. Tuscaloosa, Alabama: University of Alabama Press, 1990.

Ogden, David P. *The Fort Barrancas Story*. Washington, D. C.: Eastern National, 1997.

Parkman, Francis. *Pioneers of France in the New World*. Boston, Massachusetts: Little, Brown & Co., 1865.

Parks, Arva Moore. *Miami: The Magic City*. Tulsa, Oklahoma: Continental Heritage Press, 1981.

Parks, Joseph Howard. *General Edmund Kirby Smith, C.S.A.* Baton Rouge, Louisiana: Louisiana State University Press, 1954.

Parks, Virginia, Alan Rich and Norman Simons. *Pensacola in The Civil War*. Pensacola: Pensacola Historical Society, 1978.

Parks, Virginia and Sandra Johnson. *Civil War Views of Pensacola*. Pensacola, Florida: Pensacola Historical Society, 1993.

Patricios, Nicholas N. *Building Marvelous Miami*. Gainesville, Florida: University Press of Florida, 1994.

Patrick, Rembert W. *Florida Fiasco: Rampant Rebels on the Georgia-Florida Border, 1810-1815*. Athens, Georgia: University of Georgia Press, 1954.

Patrick, Rembert W. and Allen Morris. *Florida Under Five Flags*. Gainesville, Florida: University of Florida Press, 1967.

Pearce, George F. *Pensacola During The Civil War*. Gainesville, Florida: University Press of Florida, 2002.

Peck, Douglas T. *Ponce de Leon and the Discovery of Florida*. Bradenton, Florida: Pogo Press, 1993.

Peithmann, Irvin M. *The Unconquered Seminole Indians*. St. Petersburg, Florida: Great Outdoors Publishing Company, 1957.

Peters, Virginia Bergman. *The Florida Wars*. Hamden, Connecticut: Archon Books, 1979.

Peterson, Harold L. *Arms and Armor in Colonial America 1526-1783*. Mineola, New York: Dover Publications, 2000 (original edition published in 1956).

Pictorial History of Fort Marion. St. Augustine, Florida: W. J. Harris Company, 1925.

Pizzo, Anthony P. *Tampa Town, 1824-1886*. Miami, Florida: Hurricane House Publishers, 1968.

Postcard Guide and History of Old St. Augustine. St. Augustine, Florida: Usina's Book and Souvenir Store, 1912.

Potter, Woodburne. *The War in Florida*. Baltimore, Maryland: Lewis and Coleman, 1836.

Pratt, Fletcher. *Civil War in Pictures*. Garden City, New York: Garden City Books, 1955.

Prince, Henry. *Amidst a Storm of Bullets*. Dade City, Florida: Seminole Wars Historic Foundation, 1998.

Rawls, Carolina, editor. *The Jacksonville Story*. Jacksonville, Florida: Jacksonville Fifty Years of Progress Association, 1950.

Ray, Frederic. *St. Augustine*. Self-published, 1952.

Reavis, L.U. *The Live and Military Services of William Selby Harney*. St. Louis, Missouri: Ryan, Brand & Co., Publishers, 1878.

Reger, James P. *Life in the South During the Civil War*. San Diego, California: Lucent Books, 1997.

Reynolds, Charles B. *The Standard Guide: St. Augustine*. St. Augustine, Florida: E.H. Reynolds, 1892.

Riehecky, Janet. *The Settling of St. Augustine*. Milwaukee, Wisconsin: World Almanac Library, 2003.

Ripoll, Carlos. *St. Augustine and Cuba*. New York, New York: Editorial Dos Rios, 2002.

Robe, Jim. *Illustrated Florida History*. Self-published, 1997.

Roberts, Robert B. *Encyclopedia of Historic Forts: The Military, Pioneer and Trading Posts of the United States*. New York, New York: Macmillan Publishing Company, 1988.

Robertson, Jr., James I. *Civil War! America Becomes One Nation*. New York, New York: Alfred A. Knopf, 1992.
The Concise Illustrated History of the Civil War. Harrisburg, Pennsylvania: National Historical Society, 1979.

Robinson, Calvin L. *A Yankee in a Confederate Town*. Sarasota, Florida: Pineapple Press, 2002.

Robison, Jim and Mark Andrews. *Flashbacks: The Story of Central Florida's Past*. Orlando, Florida: *The Orlando Sentinel*, 1995.

Rogers, William Warren and Lee Willis, III. *At The Waters Edge. A Pictorial and Nararative History of Apalachicola and Franklin County*. Virginia Beach, Virginia: The Donning Company Publishers, 1997.

Ruehrwein, Richard L. *Discover Florida in The New World*. Greendale, Indiana: The Creative Company, 1997.

Sage-Gagne, Waneta. *Pilots in the Sun: Primary Pilot Training Schools in Lakeland and Avon Park, Florida 1940-1945*. Lakeland, Florida: Friends of the Library, 1990.

Schafer, Daniel L. *Thunder on the River: The Civil War in Northeast Florida*. Gainesville, Florida: University Press of Florida, 2010.

Silver, Vicki. *Back To The Water: Discovering Florida's Urban Waterfronts*. Tallahassee, Florida: Florida Department of Community Affairs, 1972.

Simons, Norman and James R. McGovern. *Pensacola in Pictures and Prints*. Pensacola, Florida: The Pensacola Series Commemorating the American Revolution Bicentennial, 1974.

Smith, Hale G. *The European and the Indian*. Gainesville, Florida: Florida Anthropological Society, 1956.

Spencer, Donald D. *Florida's Historic Forts, Camps and Battlefields*. Ormond Beach, Florida: Camelot Publishing Company, 2006.

Sprague, John T. *The Florida War*. New York, New York: Appleton & Company, 1848.
The Origin, Progress, and Conclusion of the Florida War. Gainesville, Florida: University of Florida Press, 1964.

Steele, Willard. *The Battle of Okeechobee*. Miami, Florida: Archaeological & Historical Conservancy, 1987.

Steen, Sandra and Susan Steen. *Historic St. Augustine*. Parsippany, New Jersey: Dillon Press, 1997.

Stewart, Catharine, H. B. Parramore, and E. J. Moore. *Pensacola Historical Landmarks*. Pensacola, Florida: Pensacola Historic Preservation Society, 1983.

Strutin, Michal. *Florida State Parks*. Seattle, Washington: Mountaineers Books, 2000.

Suddeth, Frank. *Fort Matanzas: 1742*. St. Augustine, Florida: Self-published, 1997.

Sweeney, James B. *A Pictorial Guide to the Military Museums, Forts and Historic Sites of the United States*. New York, New York: Crown Publishers, Inc., 1981.

Tampa Bay History, Vol. 11, No. 1. Tampa, Florida: University of South Florida, 1989.

Taylor, Paul. *Discovering The Civil War In Florida*. Sarasota, Florida: Pineapple Press, 2001.

The Spirit of Naval Aviation. Pensacola, Florida: Naval Aviation Museum Foundation, Inc., 2002.

Thomas, Dean S. *Cannons: An Introduction to Civil War Artillery*. Gettysburg, Pennsylvania: Thomas Publications, 1985.

Tricebock, Kenneth F. *Explore Sarasota and Vicinity*. Self-published, 1986.
Historic Sites and Buildings. Self-published, 1996.

Utley, Robert M. and Wilcomb E. Washburn. *The Indian Wars*. New York, New York: American Heritage Publishing Company, 1977.

Van Campen, J. T. *St. Augustine: Florida's Colonial Capital*. St. Augustine, Florida: St. Augustine Historical Society, 1959.

Varner, John Grier and Jeannette Johnson Varner. *The Florida of The Inca*. Austin, Texas: University of Texas Press, 1951.

Vest, Jr., Banks B. and Elizabeth B. Ratliff. *Florida: Arrows To Astronauts*. Tampa, Florida: Beach Products, Inc.,

1969.

Voldbrecht, John L. *Castillo: The Dramatic Story of Spain's Great 17th Century Fortress in Saint Augustine*. St. Augustine, Florida: J. Carver Harris, 1949.

Wade, Linda R. *St. Augustine: America's Oldest City*. Vero Beach, Florida: Rourke Enterprises, Inc., 1991.

Wagman, Jules L. *Jacksonville and Florida's First Coast*. Northridge, California: Windsor Publications, 1988.

Wallace, John. *Carpetbag Rule in Florida, 1888*. Gainesville, Florida: University of Florida Press, 1964.

Walton, Chelle Koster. *Florida*. New York, New York: Compass American Guides, 2003.

Ward, James Robertson. *Old Hickory's Town*. Jacksonville, Florida: Florida Publishing Company, 1982.

Weaver II, John R. *A Legacy in Brick and Stone: American Coastal Defense Forts of the Third System, 1816-1867*. McLean, Viginia: Redoubt Press, 2001.

Weisman, Brent Richards. *Unconquered People, Florida's Seminole and Miccosukee Indians*. Gainesville, Florida: University Press of Florida, 1999.

Whitman, Sylvia. *Hernando de Soto and the Explorers of the American South*. New York, New York: Chelsea House Publishers, 1991.

Wickman, Patricia Riles. *Osceola's Legacy*. Tuscaloosa, Alabama: University of Alabama Press, 1991.

Wiles, Jon W. *Invisible Saint Augustine*. St. Augustine, Florida: Self-published, 1992.

Williams, Charles J. *The Peninsular State Story*. Jacksonville, Florida: Peninsular Life Insurance Company, 1958.

Williams, Lindsey Wilger. *Boldly Onward*. Charlotte Harbor, Florida: Precision Publishing Co., 1986.

Wolf, John B. *The Battle at the Loxahatchee River: The Seminole War*. Jupiter, Florida: Loxahatchee Historical Society, 1989.

Wood, Wayne W. *Jacksonville's Architectural Heritage*. Gainesville, Florida: University Press of Florida, 1989.

Wright, Jr., J. Leitch. *Florida in the American Revolution*. Gainesville, Florida: University Presses of Florida, 1975.

Wyllie, H.S. *St. Augustine Under Flags*. St. Augustine, Florida: St. Augustine Record Company, 1898.

Wynne, Lewis N. editor. *Florida At War*. Saint Leo, Florida: Saint Leo College Press, 1993.

Wynne, Lewis N. and Robert A. Taylor. *Florida In The Civil War*. Charleston, South Carolina: Arcadia Publishing, 2001.

Zitsman, Charles, editor. *Adventure Florida's First Coast*. St. Augustine, Florida: St. George Publishing, 1994.

Index